LIVING FOR
JESUS
WITH
ADHD

JAKE HICKENBOTTOM

© 2024 by Jason Hickenbottom

No part of this book may be reproduced, stored in a retrieval system, or transmitted in any form or by any means—electronic, mechanical, photocopy, recording, or otherwise—without prior written permission of the publisher, except for brief quotations in critical reviews or articles. Unauthorized reproduction, distribution, or sale of this publication is prohibited and may be subject to legal action.

Unless otherwise stated, all Scripture quotations are from the ESV Bible (The Holy Bible, English Standard Version), copyright © 2001 by Crossway, a publishing ministry of Good News Publishers. Used by permission. All rights reserved.

Unless otherwise stated for distribution in countries outside the United States, all printing manufactured in the USA

Published by Production ONE Ministries
Production ONE Ministries
P.O. Box 3013
2001 N. Mattis Ave.
Champaign IL, 61826

ISBN: 979-8-218-47627-4

Edited by Shelly Manning
Cover and Page Art by Teja Hickenbottom

Email | info@production-one.com
Website | www.production-one.com

For my children Lincoln and Lily

"May this book be a legacy to our family through the generations. May it be a guide to generations of our family that I will never meet."

The greatest joy in my life is being your Father.

-Love, Dad

CONTENTS

	Forward	Pg. 9
	Introduction	Pg. 15
1.	Embracing ADHD with Faith	Pg. 25
2.	The Holy Spirit, Creativity, and ADHD	Pg. 37
3.	Journey Towards the Spirit of Rejection	Pg. 53
4.	Battling Isolation and Identity	Pg. 71
5.	Identity Crisis	Pg. 85
6.	Transition into High School	Pg. 97
7.	Upper Classman Years	Pg. 113
8.	Senior Year	Pg. 133
9.	New Life as a Christian	Pg. 145
10.	A Determined Path to Eastern Illinois University	Pg. 161
11.	Starting Fresh	Pg. 179
12.	From Chains to Freedom	Pg. 205
	References	Pg. 223
	Sponsors	Pg. 227

FOREWORD

BY

PUTTY PUTMAN

Foreword

Jake Hickenbottom and I first crossed paths around 2017. He began attending a church where I was serving on the pastoral team, and shortly thereafter, he attended School of Kingdom Ministry, a training school I led to equip people in a lifestyle of Holy Spirit ministry.

At that point I had been operating School of Kingdom Ministry for about seven years. It was incredibly exciting; God had breathed on our little school and it was spreading to churches across the country, and even around the world. I was racing to keep up with all the growth. Extra layers were coming along - exciting, but complex layers - with a growing travel ministry, writing books, and more. It was amazing, but intense. Exhilarating and exhausting. When Jake took the class, I had been on this ever-speeding-up roller coaster for many years, and I was getting tired.

I didn't know it until later, but the Lord spoke to Jake and told him to help keep my life fun. He began inviting me to events and activities that were a welcome lifeline for me in many ways. Game nights, taking our kids to a children's museum, enjoying unique restaurants in our area. At the time, my fun tank was dangerously low, and Jake had a very significant ministry to me in that regard. It wasn't a ministry that many knew was happening (though Jake knew), and it strengthened me in ways that surprised me. I really don't know how I would have made it through those intense years without Jake's ministry of friendship and amusement.

Needless to say, this was the beginning of many adventures together. Together, we have visited the world's largest arcade (twice), climbed mountains, prayed through work and family issues, helped each other move, brainstormed ministry ideas, and much more. Along the way we've had lots of laughs and loads of good food. That friendship continues, even though we now live a few thousand miles apart.

Throughout the course of our friendship, it has been clear to me that Jake's mind works differently than mine. Jake's life experiences are unlike my experiences. Of course there is a normal degree to which everyone's experience of life is unique, but Jake's stands apart from mine in a more significant way, and it's been interesting to see that up close through our friendship. I'm no expert on ADHD, but it seems obvious to me that the circuits are wired differently in Jake's mind than they are in mine. The way his attention flows and what comes out of that flow adheres to a different pattern than mine does. ADHD is a central part of his experience of himself, as I imagine it is for everyone who shares that diagnosis.

What I have come to appreciate about Jake and his journey with ADHD is the way he sees it as an avenue of connection with God. It would be easy to process a diagnosis like ADHD as something that acts as an obstacle in his walk with God. "Why am I different than everyone else, Lord?" I haven't seen Jake do that. Rather than resisting the life he has, including the ADHD-informed shape of his experience, Jake assumes that he can meet God in it. What if it is an avenue of finding God rather than an obstacle to be navigated? I just love that perspective and it's been powerful to see the fruit of that approach in his life.

A while ago, Jake asked me a vulnerable question, and one that made me really reflect. He asked, "Do you think I'll have ADHD in eternity?" As I contemplated his question, I noted my inclination to say probably not, but then I found myself nudged with this thought: I wonder how different my experience of my mind will be as well? Could it be that my experience of my own mind will be no less different than Jake's? There is something that rings true in that to me. Whether we share a diagnosis with Jake or not, our experience of ourselves now is but a shadow of what it will be in eternity. This means that all of us relate to God from a significantly incomplete vantage point mentally. The best any of us can do is to seek God the best we can to the best of our capacities right now, and allow the life we believe to be a vehicle that God uses to make Himself known to us.

That is precisely what Jake does in these pages: he reveals the way God has spoken through the life he has, and the ways he's coming to know God in it. He peels back the curtain and shares authentically what his journey has been. The highs and lows, the valleys God has met him in, and the mountain tops he has celebrated upon. In it all, I came to appreciate a little more fully what it would be like to have ADHD. Beyond that, I came to appreciate the God who yet again makes Himself known to us afresh. I believe this book will be a valuable investment for anyone whose life has been impacted by ADHD, and I know you'll be blessed for reading it!

Putty Putman
Pastor, Author

INTRODUCTION

Introduction

What is ADHD?

Attention-deficit/hyperactivity disorder (ADHD) is one of the most common neurobehavioral disorders of childhood. It is sometimes referred to as Attention Deficit Disorder (ADD). It is usually first diagnosed in childhood and often lasts into adulthood. Children with ADHD may have trouble paying attention, controlling impulsive behaviors (may act without thinking about what the result will be), or be overly active.

The World vs. ADHD

I wish I could tell you all you need to know about ADHD. I wish I could tell you my journey with ADHD has been easy. Simply put, ADHD is .... (sigh) .... complicated. ADHD...

Attention Deficit Hyperactive Disorder. Any person that hears this acronym will most likely associate it with someone that has a diagnosis of ADHD. You may have a memory of an uncle with ADHD. Maybe you're a parent about to get a diagnosis for your child and praying that it is not ADHD. Perhaps you're a teacher and must educate a student with ADHD. No matter what your association is with ADHD, chances are, it is complicated.

While spending time in prayer, I came to a revelation. ADHD is complicated but straightforward to those who have it. Moreover, I see now how this plays out in our current society. There are two worldviews that could relate to that statement: "Not having ADHD" and "Having ADHD."

Let's consider that you do not have ADHD, and you go about your life looking from the outside in. Hypothetically, let's say that two of your best friends want to hang out. One has ADHD and tends to be disruptive, interrupts conversations, and their mind never seems to stay focused on the current conversation. As the friendship develops over time, you begin to ask yourself, "Why is my friend acting this way?" "Do they see or understand that we don't want this behavior in our relationship?" Welcome to the worldview of not having ADHD. What's happening here is that the person with ADHD does not understand your perspective. You have your worldview of living without ADHD, while your friend's worldview is that they live with ADHD, and this is simply the way they are.

In my experience, the worldview of not having ADHD prevails. Since ADHD is not considered the norm in our society, those without the diagnosis often establish social norms without considering the experiences of those living with ADHD. Due to this worldview, society tends to favor quick fixes, treatments, or permanent cures for ADHD.

Now, I would like to flip the roles and give you the perspective of a person who has ADHD. Let's say that two of your best friends want to hang out. You have ADHD, and they do not. When you are with your friends, you feel very excited and passionate about the friendship. The conversations excite you and you start to contribute by telling stories that relate to theirs. However, your friends begin to ignore you because your interjections seem out of place. This frustrates you. At this point, you want to be heard, so you interject your thoughts during a lively conversation. Your friends get upset, and eventually, the relationship suffers. You reach out to your friends and discover that they are hanging out without you. Over time, they have pushed you away. At this point, feelings of rejection start to take root in your life.

Here is the reality of the situation: Friends without ADHD may get burned out and not want to deal with the behavior of someone who has it. The two friends still care for and love you, but they choose not to be around you as much. To you (or the person with ADHD), this can feel like a downward spiral because there is no explanation for why it is happening. The truth is that the person living with ADHD strives to live up to what society expects. ADHD is normal to them, but not to most people. Often, those with ADHD will struggle with quick fixes such as medication or a "chill pill." They are desperate to be accepted and try to appear "normal," but are unable to change their behavior because they may not be aware of what is happening in their brain. They may also be unaware of how to change their actions or where to go for help. I know this because I have been undergoing treatment for ADHD for over 30 years. There are amazing doctors out there who genuinely want to help those living with ADHD. In other words, I would not be in a position today to write a book if it were not for my doctor.

Adapting to Christian Life with ADHD

Early in my Christian Walk, I would often pray to be delivered and cured of ADHD. To this day, I have never been. One question I am frequently asked is, "Can I be cured of ADHD?" I am going to be bold and say that I have never seen it. However, partnering with the Holy Spirit and reading the teachings of the Bible, I have found peace in many areas where ADHD is a problem for me. Throughout this book, I will break down simple and practical applications using the Bible to help you or your loved one manage ADHD. Keep in mind, this is no quick fix, and it takes real and intentional effort. As you read this book, I hope you will gain a better understanding of ADHD to share with the world. I hope you are able to grow with a new and fresh look at ADHD. The world cannot cure ADHD, but we certainly can better ourselves by partnering with God and change the world's view of ADHD.

Something happened in the summer of 2016 that changed my life forever: God began to speak to me through the Holy Spirit, and let me tell you, it was awesome! I started to learn that ADHD is a complicated tool. You must learn how to use it. You must understand it to its core, know its strengths and weaknesses, and how it can affect others.

Growing up in a family of carpenters, my father and grandfather taught me the ropes of carpentry. I learned how to drive a nail into a piece of lumber, how to use a power saw effectively, and I even learned how to correct my mistakes. In reality, no one is proficient at something from the start. Everything must be learned.

So, what does all this mean? While there may not be a cure for ADHD, there is a solution. According to the Bible, we are called to be good stewards of our minds. Learning to live properly with ADHD means that I must include the Holy Spirit and my relationship with God in the mix in order to live a fulfilling life.

Set your minds on things that are above, not on things that are on earth.

Colossians 3:2

"Therefore, preparing your minds for action, and being sober-minded, set your hope fully on the grace that will be brought to you at the revelation of Jesus Christ."

1 Peter 1:13

Getting Started with Writing

It was December 2017. I was attending a local church's Saturday night service when I heard the Holy Spirit speak to me about reflecting on my past—living with ADHD. I thought about the many struggles I had and began to break them down with God. Dissecting each matter was like opening a new

Introduction

book filled with ideas. God started to point out how He was involved in each situation even though I did not see it at the time. He would show me verses in the book of Proverbs that King Solomon wrote, suggesting, "What if you applied this scripture to that situation?" Having this experience gave me hope, and I wanted to share that hope with others. In that moment, I made up my mind. I would start writing about my life experiences with ADHD and explore biblical theology on how to improve them. I realized that I cannot change my past, but I can share my mistakes and experiences with others so that they, too, can discover how to use biblical principles as solutions to the problems stemming from ADHD.

As I began to embark on this journey, I started looking for other books involving ADHD, God, and the Bible. I found a few. However, I felt there was nothing that spoke the truth concerning ADHD and the Holy Spirit. The world needs to know how God's greatest gift to humanity—the Holy Spirit—can positively impact your life, whether you or a loved one is living with ADHD. I want to make one thing very clear, though. This book is about identity in Jesus and dealing with ADHD, being empowered by, and learning how to use ADHD as God intended. I aim to show scriptural truths about my own experiences and bring to life new and practical ways to handle these ADHD situations.

Here is the truth. The Bible states that I am created in God's image. "So, God created man in his own image, in the image of God he created him; male and female he created them." (Genesis 1:27)

So, I challenged God with a question about being created in His image. God answered my challenge. My encounter was not some Hollywood-style voice of God you hear in the movies. It was simply a time of prayer and hearing what the Father had to say. Here is how it went down.

- **Me:** God, why do I think so many thoughts at once? Why am I not able to focus more narrowly?

- **God:** Do you think (long pause) that I think (long pause) about just one thing at a time?
- **Me:** Um, well, you have a point. If I am to think many thoughts at once, why am I not able to focus well?

- **God:** Be holy in your mind (long pause) and be a good steward of your thoughts.

The conversation ended at that point. I was floored by the response! My whole life, I have lived with this so-called "ADHD," as if something was wrong with me, and that I was supposed to try to act "NORMAL." My whole worldview on ADHD changed that day. The truth is, "NOTHING IS WRONG WITH ME!" Denying who I was created to be is wrong and doesn't please God. The standard worldview of ADHD is a lie from Satan. With that revelation, I understood that Satan wants to imprison people with ADHD, persecute them for who they are, and cast a false identity upon them.

So, if you are a single parent dealing with an ADHD child, or a middle-aged man being diagnosed with ADHD for the first time, this book is for you. It is not a quick answer guide to a multiple-choice test on ADHD. The truth is, I do not have all the answers. ADHD is real, and it has real impacts, both negative and positive. So, from the bottom of my heart, I thank you for picking up this book to hear my story. I hope this inspires you to make a change in the world while living with ADHD.

To the single parent dealing with a child who has ADHD, I say to you: take on the challenge of unlocking your child's true identity so that they may love themselves as God loves them. And to the middle-aged man being diagnosed with ADHD for the first time, know that you are not disqualified, and your situation does not define you. Come on, Holy Spirit! Let's shake the very foundations of ADHD. May God bless your journey as you read this book. I pray in Jesus' mighty name that you be moved to make a change in this world.

CHAPTER ONE

EMBRACING ADHD

WITH FAITH

CHAPTER ONE

EMBRACING ADHD
WITH FAITH

Chapter One

Embracing ADHD with Faith

Everyone has a story to tell, but no story is simple. Even stories told by two people from the same event will be different. Why is that? I often reflect on the differences that any two people might have. This reflection materializes especially when it is related to ADHD. I have found there are many overlapping similarities between two people with ADHD, even though the individuals are very different.

As you continue reading, I want to share my story from my point of view, to let you experience my life events, and to see them as I did. It is not natural to look back 30+ years and recall specific details about my life. As you journey ahead through this book, I will be lifting the veil on my childhood. I will tell you things that not even my closest friends and family know. My experiences are my own and will only be presented from my perspective. If you want to have a better understanding of ADHD, I encourage you to view my story through your own lens. In other words, try to relate my story to your own ADHD situation. "King David wrote songs and psalms to the Lord asking, "Teach me your paths."

"Make me to know your ways, O Lord; teach me your paths. Lead me in your truth and teach me, for you are the God of my salvation; for you I will wait all the day long."

Psalm 25: 4-5

In this psalm, David is seeking wisdom on how to discern the path God wants him to follow. As you begin this first chapter, I encourage you to emulate King David: pray and seek God, waiting on Him to guide your understanding. Holy Spirit, please show up and grant understanding to all who journey through this book.

Where it all Began

It was 1989. I was eight years old, a typical third grader with lots of energy, in a new school with new friends. My life was good. I had no worries at all. No cell phones, no Internet—just simple electronics to hold our attention. We were community-driven and eager to experience life together. On warm days, I would play baseball with my friends, and on rainy ones, I'd power on my Nintendo to play video games with my brother. Life was fun and straightforward, no real troubles to speak of. However, that year things took a turn that would make an impact on me for nothing less than the rest of my life. This was the year I was diagnosed with ADHD.

In order to get a full diagnosis, doctors had to complete several tests. My mom and I took many trips to Carle Hospital in Urbana, Illinois, which was about an hour's drive from my home in Charleston. I never really asked questions about the trips because my mom took me out to eat at some amazing restaurants that we didn't have back home, and I got to visit the mega toy store there. When I was getting tested, I didn't know why or what they were doing. I remember having a brain scan done using flashes of light, answering a series of questions, and listening in on conversations between my mom and the doctor. I remember asking my parents, "What is ADHD?" My dad simply said, "You can't sit still." At the time, this did not mean anything to me. I just went about my life, doing the things I always did.

After several visits to Carle Hospital and finally receiving a diagnosis of ADHD, I found myself in the kitchen with both of my parents. They had a bottle of pills and my favorite bowl. I asked my parents "why is my Teenage Mutant Ninja Turtle bowl out on the counter?" My mother replied "Your Dad and I know you love this bowl and that it is your favorite. Since the bowl is so different than all our other bowls, we would like to use it to inspire you to take your new ADHD medication." I immediately was confused and walked over to the bowl. Inside the bowl was a pill called Ritalin. I had never swallowed a pill before. "Do I have to swallow it? Can't I chew it?" I protested. "I don't want to swallow it!" My dad became frustrated but nonetheless, he bribed me with an incentive of $20.00 if I swallowed the pill. "Okay," I said. My dad then handed me a beverage, and I embarked on my first attempt at swallowing a pill.

Thirty minutes later, I found myself feeling not just somewhat different, but a whole lot different! My mind became unlocked in a way I had never experienced before. My brain started processing information in a way that was different from my usual approach. My usually non-linear mindset suddenly shifted to a linear one. I began to notice that I had incredible focus and mental energy. Ritalin had become the new wonder drug to calm kids down and help them achieve what they could not do on their own. Society now had its first label for hyperactive kids: ADHD. They had found a way to treat it using prescribed stimulants.

Grade School Life

After starting my medication, I went about my daily life as a third-grade student. The bell rang. RECESS TIME! It is no secret that recess is the best time of the day. We all lined up and went outside. As I was playing with my friends, my third-grade teacher pulled me aside. I thought to myself, "Am I in trouble for something?" But this time, it was different from what I expected.

My teacher asked, "What is ADHD?" I honestly had no answer for her. I don't remember what I said, but she proceeded to ask another question: "Do you feel the medicine is helping?" At the time, all I wanted to do was go back and play with my friends. "I think it does," I replied. "Never mind, "she said, so I went back and played with my friends.

I often think back to this event that took place in my life over 30 years ago. What was going on here? Did my teacher ask a question because she didn't know or understand? She noticed a difference in my behavior and had questions about it. To my knowledge, I was one of the few students diagnosed with ADHD and taking medication to aid my classroom behavior. Something was working for me, and my ability to focus had improved. As a result, teachers were taking notice. Hence, the "wonder drug" seemed to be the answer.

As I began to adapt to everyday life while being medicated for ADHD, something inside me started to feel uneasy. It was a sensation in the back of my mind that something was wrong. Little did I know or understand at the time, but the Holy Spirit was speaking to me. As I grew older, this voice intensified. Not only the voice, but also the feeling in my heart and gut grew. It was the feeling of being controlled, and at the same time, I felt I was missing something in life. Shame and guilt were building up. I was growing up not being who God had created me to be. It was as if two versions of myself began to form. The medicated version of myself developed habits that could only be attained in the medicated state. My unmedicated state would have to try hard to keep up with these habits. Thus, a dependency on my medication formed. One side of the coin could do things the other side could not, and vice versa.

As I grew into high school, specifically in my junior and senior years, relationships became more complicated. My friends started to have a more difficult time with me outside of school. To make things worse, I chose not to take my Ritalin after school, which caused relational issues when interacting with my friends. My behavior would shift; I became someone who couldn't sit still and was easily distracted. I was someone who didn't quite fit into society's norm. Because of this, I found it hard to keep friends in high school. Looking back now, I can see the real problem. The Holy Spirit was speaking to me and was trying to warn me. You see, the unmedicated me as a senior in high school was actually my third-grade younger self. WHAT??? Yes, this is hard to understand but hear me out. The story started with a third-grade boy learning how to deal with life as God created him to be.

Being introduced to a drug that changed my behavior, the medicated younger me grew up conforming to society's norms. In contrast, the unmedicated boy did not. I failed to learn self-love or to fully embrace my unique identity as God created me. Jesus' greatest commandment was to love others as He loved, and this includes loving oneself.

"This is my commandment, that you love one another as I have loved you."

John 15:12

When Jesus was asked which commandment is the most important to all he responded:

"The most important is, 'Hear, O Israel: The Lord our God, the Lord is one. And you shall love the Lord your God with all your heart and with all your soul and with all your mind and with all your strength.' The second is this: 'You shall love your neighbor as yourself.' There is no other commandment greater than these."- *Mark 12:29-31*

The correlation here is that if you do not love yourself, you will treat others as you treat yourself. Loving God with all your heart and loving yourself enables you to love others well. Not loving myself created real, life-changing problems for me moving forward—how I handled relationships, interacted with family, and engaged with teachers. The struggle with focusing became even worse when I did not love myself. However, a breakthrough in medication and the support of a fantastic doctor (whom I still see) helped me navigate severe focus issues and other areas of my life. While medication improved my ability to focus and succeed in life, it did not teach me self-love. Reflecting on my journey, I asked myself: "Is this the right way? How do I cope with not loving myself because of ADHD?" Many people have posed similar questions to me in my adult life. My answer is simple: Do what works for your ADHD situation. If you're a parent with an ADHD child, pray, seek guidance, then do what is best for your child. This principle also applies to adults with ADHD. Embrace self-love and stewardship of who God created you to be. Be the best *YOU*, loving yourself both on and off medication.

Instructions for Making a Choice for Your ADHD Decision

Making an ADHD-related choice for your child, a loved one, or even yourself is complicated. It is ugly, and nothing about ADHD comes easy when discerning what is right. I am going to challenge you, though. Here are some simple steps to follow when you need answers:

- Find a quiet place.

- Be still in your mind.

- Invite the presence of the Holy Spirit.

- In peaceful stillness, begin to hear the voice of the Holy Spirit.

- Ask God the Father for wisdom on your ADHD situation.

- Invite Jesus to show you how to live with that ADHD decision.

- Most importantly, write down what was spoken to you by the Holy Spirit. Journaling is a fantastic tool to go back and reflect on.

- Finally, do it! If you hesitate or change your mind, you will miss out on all the love and grace that God wants to show you in your situation with ADHD.

If you do this, and with the correct heart posture, I know the presence of God will help you make the best choice. There is so much wisdom that God wants to show us about making the right decisions in our lives, even with ADHD. In the Bible, the book of Proverbs speaks of trusting the Lord with all your heart.

"Let not steadfast love and faithfulness forsake you; bind them around your neck; write them on the tablet of your heart. So you will find favor and good success in the sight of God and man. Trust in the Lord with all your heart, and do not lean on your own understanding. In all ways acknowledge him, and he will make straight your paths."

Proverbs 3:3-6

I encourage all who follow these steps to first meditate on the above verses. After inviting the Holy Spirit into your stillness, continue pressing into the Lord without allowing distractions. Embrace the quiet space of peace. Approach this time not with a mindset of solitude or isolation, but with utter dependence on hearing the voice of God alone. Once you reach that place, proceed to ask questions about your ADHD situation.

Evangelist and author Robby Dawkins once said, "His voice and promptings are often as light as a feather landing on your arm. It would be easy to brush it off and ignore it." Ensure that emotional thoughts do not distract you from feeling that gentle touch.

Embracing ADHD as part of God's divine design invites you to explore the unique ways in which this condition shapes your spiritual and personal journey. Recognizing ADHD as an integral part of God's plan enhances your understanding of His love and purpose for you. This acceptance is not just about acknowledging your challenges but also appreciating the distinctive strengths that ADHD brings into your life.

Key Takeaways

1. **Understanding ADHD as Part of God's Creation:** Acknowledge that ADHD is woven into God's purposeful design for you. Viewing ADHD through this lens allows you to see it as a significant part of your divine identity, crafted by God.

2. **Embracing Jesus Christ's Teachings for Growth:** Embrace your journey with ADHD by grounding it in the teachings of Jesus Christ. This connection provides a robust framework for understanding and coping with ADHD spiritually.

3. **Acceptance through the Love of God:** Foster acceptance of your ADHD by recognizing it as part of God's creation. Biblical teachings affirm that every aspect of your being is made with divine intention, enhancing your sense of self-worth and belonging.

4. **Incorporating Biblical Principles and the Holy Spirit in Daily Life:** Use the guidance of the Holy Spirit and the principles found in the Bible to manage ADHD. This includes regular prayer, meditation on scripture, and seeking the Holy Spirit's wisdom in everyday challenges.

Personal Story Reflection

- **Sharing Your Story:** After reading about my journey with ADHD and faith, take a moment to reflect on your own ADHD journey. What has been the most challenging aspect of ADHD for you? What has been the most rewarding?

- **Faith's Role:** How has faith influenced your approach to managing ADHD? Write down instances where you felt divine guidance or support in your struggles or successes.

Exercise - Identifying Strengths and Challenges

1. List out five strengths that you believe ADHD has given you—these could be creativity, resilience, the ability to think quickly on your feet, etc.
2. Next, list out five challenges that come with your ADHD.
3. Reflect on how your faith has helped you leverage your strengths and address your challenges. Consider writing a prayer or affirmation that acknowledges these strengths and asks for support in areas of challenge.

Interactive Journal

For the next week, keep a daily gratitude journal. Each day, write down at least one thing related to your ADHD for which you are grateful. This could be a personal trait, a relationship that has been formed or strengthened through your ADHD journey, or an unexpected opportunity that arose from an ADHD-driven experience.

Prayer

1. Start by thanking God for the unique way He has created you, including your ADHD.
2. Ask for peace and acceptance of yourself and your diagnosis.
3. Pray for understanding from friends, family, and colleagues.
4. Seek guidance on how to use your ADHD as a tool for creativity, service, and witness.

CHAPTER TWO

THE HOLY SPIRIT, CREATIVITY, AND ADHD

Chapter Two

The Holy Spirit, Creativity, and ADHD

Navigating ADHD through Research, Divergent Thinking, and the Holy Spirit

In this chapter, we'll journey into research that provides a comprehensive understanding of ADHD, laying the foundation for the topics explored throughout the book. Drawing upon esteemed research outlets and medical journals, I will delve into concepts like divergent thinking and hyperfocus while weaving in my own experiences and beliefs. This chapter will offer unique insights and perspectives on ADHD that might be new to you.

Divergent Thinking: The Creative Pathway of ADHD

One concept you might already know is divergent thinking—a thought process involving the exploration of numerous solutions and perspectives to generate creative ideas. It breaks conventional thinking patterns, allowing individuals to produce innovative ideas and solutions. In my experience as someone with ADHD, divergent thinking forms the baseline of how we think. Our ability to swiftly come up with original ideas may seem peculiar to others, but it's simply a part of our natural approach to problem-solving. Adaptability and quick thinking often guide us, sometimes at the expense of efficiency, yet frequently yielding effective results.

Aspect	Typical Thinking	Divergent Thinking in ADHD
Definition	Linear, follows logical steps	Explores multiple, unrelated ideas simultaneously
Problem Solving	Seeks a single correct answer	Generates creative solutions and multiple answers
Creativity	Often constrained by norms	Highly original and less bound by conventional rules
Focus	Consistent and steady	Variable, influenced by interest
Outcome	Predictable results	Innovative and unexpected results

Hyperfocus: Harnessing Deep Concentration

The next topic I would like to address is hyperfocus, a state of intense concentration on a task or activity that leads to a loss of awareness of time and surroundings. Throughout my career in Information Technology (IT), I have seen many software developers strive to attain this level of focus. For me, as someone with ADHD, hyperfocus happens naturally when I'm deeply engrossed in an area of interest. However, this intense focus can overshadow other priorities, so I often need to train my mind to disengage. Without such control, interruptions or shifting priorities can result in frustration.

When someone with ADHD is in this state, it's best to let them be, as interruptions can lead to agitation and frustration. The focus is so strong that breaking it can seem disrespectful or insensitive. For children with ADHD, it's crucial to nurture their understanding of hyperfocus as a gift rather than an impediment. They should learn how to transition in and out of hyperfocus, understanding that leaving this state does not mean they are ignoring other important matters. Inattentiveness can often be mistaken for a lack of attention. But in reality, their creative thinking or deep focus may have guided them elsewhere.

Focus Type	Description	Advantages	Challenges
Hyperfocus (ADHD)	Intense concentration on a task	High productivity in short bursts; deep immersion in topics of interest	Neglecting other tasks; difficulty switching tasks
Typical Focus	Regular attention control	Balanced attention across tasks; easier task switching	May lack deep concentration on a single task

The Holy Spirit: Guiding Influence and Source of Creativity

The third subject explored in this chapter is the Holy Spirit, a gift from God after the resurrection of Jesus Christ. The book of Acts provides more details, so I encourage you to read it to learn more. Fundamentally, the Holy Spirit was bestowed upon believers who proclaimed the resurrection. For me, the Holy Spirit profoundly influences my thinking, behavior, and actions. In 2024, my primary aim was to remain attuned to God's direction through the guidance of the Holy Spirit, which required continual relational growth with God.

Listening to God isn't solely about hearing words—it often involves emotions and a sense of presence. Through this connection, I can enter hyperfocus and divergent thinking, discovering creative solutions and ideas.

As we transition into the research section, please note that the information presented is supported by reputable sources. I hope this chapter illuminates the relationship between ADHD, divergent thinking, hyperfocus, and relational growth with God, offering practical insights for individuals and families alike.

Element	Influence on ADHD	Role of the Holy Spirit
Creativity	Enhanced divergent thinking	Inspires and directs creative energies
Focus	Hyperfocus can be a blessing and a challenge	Provides guidance to manage focus and use it constructively
Emotional Regulation	Often challenging for those with ADHD	Offers comfort and helps manage emotions
Life Purpose	Searching for meaning and direction	Encourages purposeful living and spiritual growth

Research Explained

When looking at the relationship between the Holy Spirit, ADHD, and creativity, we are navigating a landscape that touches on theology, psychology, and the arts. The Holy Spirit, in Christian theology, is often associated with inspiration, guidance, and the empowerment of individuals to achieve beyond their natural capacities. He is seen as a source of divine inspiration that can lead to extraordinary creativity and insight, providing believers with a deeper sense of purpose and the ability to express divine truths through their talents and abilities. For me, the Holy Spirit is God's spirit living inside us as believers. The Holy Spirit enters believers who have accepted Jesus Christ as their savior and believe in His resurrection from the dead. For a more in depth look at the Holy Spirit read the book of Acts in the Bible.

ADHD, on the other hand, is a neurodevelopment disorder characterized by symptoms such as inattention, hyperactivity, and impulsivity. While these traits can pose challenges in certain areas of life, research and anecdotal evidence suggest that individuals with ADHD can also display remarkable creativity and innovative thinking. Their ability to think outside the box, hyperfocus on subjects of interest, and generate a wealth of ideas can be seen as strengths, particularly in creative endeavors. Research and anecdotal evidence suggest a nuanced relationship between ADHD and creativity, offering valuable insights into how individuals with ADHD can leverage their unique cognitive styles for creative endeavors. A study featured in Frontiers in Psychology found a positive association between ADHD symptoms and divergent thinking in a population without ADHD diagnosis. This suggests that ADHD traits can contribute to creative problem-solving abilities. This relationship was characterized by increased fluency, flexibility, and originality in divergent thinking, particularly tied to inattention symptoms of ADHD. The study also discussed the potential of a broad attentional focus, common in ADHD, to facilitate originality and flexibility by perceiving more and different external stimuli, which could enhance creative outputs.

Psychology Today shared personal narratives underscoring the creative advantages of ADHD. For instance, divergent thinking, often seen in ADHD, can lead to original and imaginative problem-solving abilities. One example provided is of a child combining interests in origami and space technologies to design a vehicle for Mars exploration. The story highlighted how ADHD can enhance capabilities in music, art, and computational thinking, leading to inventive problem-solving.

Furthermore, a review in CHADD's Attention Magazine of 31 studies on ADHD and creativity revealed mixed findings but suggested a general trend: real-world creativity and divergent thinking abilities may be stronger among adults with ADHD, especially outside clinical settings. The review indicated that ADHD could be linked to higher achievements in creative domains in daily life, although the relationship between ADHD and convergent thinking (problem-solving that follows a set of rules to find an optimal solution) appears to be less clear or even negative.

These findings collectively suggest that while ADHD can pose challenges, it may also bestow unique cognitive abilities that enhance creative thinking and real-world creative achievements. The positive association between ADHD symptoms and divergent thinking capabilities underscores the potential for individuals with ADHD to excel in creative endeavors, particularly when they can harness their natural inclinations toward innovation and out-of-the-box thinking.

The connection between the Holy Spirit and creativity, when considered in the context of ADHD, opens an interesting dialogue. Individuals with ADHD may experience a unique form of inspiration and creativity that aligns with the concept of divine guidance or the work of the Holy Spirit. This is very true in my life today as a follower of Jesus Christ. The natural inclination toward innovative thinking and problem-solving can be viewed as a gift or talent that, when nurtured within a spiritual framework, can lead to profound expressions of faith and creativity. Moreover, the challenges associated with ADHD, such as navigating a world that is often structured around linear thinking and traditional productivity assessment, can lead to a deepened reliance on faith and the Holy Spirit for guidance, strength, and a sense of belonging. This reliance can foster a unique artistic or creative voice that reflects an individual's journey with both their faith and their neurodivergence. In the arts, many individuals have attributed their creative inspiration to a combination of their unique neurological makeup and a sense of spiritual calling or divine inspiration. This synergy between the Holy Spirit, ADHD, and creativity suggests that the relationship between our neurological diversity, spiritual life, and creative expression is complex and deeply personal. It invites a broader conversation about how we understand talent, inspiration, and the ways in which our differences contribute to the richness of our human experience. In summary, the interplay between the Holy Spirit, ADHD, and creativity highlights the diverse ways in which individuals experience and express their faith, their neurodivergence, and their creative gifts. It underscores the importance of recognizing and valuing the unique perspectives and talents that each person brings to the table, and the potential for profound creativity and insight that can emerge from the intersection of spirituality and neurodiversity.

Hyperfocus

Hyperfocus is indeed a fascinating and often beneficial aspect of ADHD, allowing individuals to engage deeply with tasks or subjects that interest them. This capability, while not without its challenges, can result in impressive bursts of productivity, creativity, and innovation. In certain contexts, the deep immersion and intense concentration experienced during hyperfocus can be likened to a form of spiritual or divine inspiration, especially when it leads to the creation of something deeply meaningful or transformative.

To better understand what hyperfocus is, I am going to break it down into five categories and further explain each of them.

- **Nature of Hyperfocus:** It's like a laser beam of concentration, where external distractions fade away, and one's entire being is invested in the task at hand. This can be particularly advantageous in creative pursuits, research, or any activity that benefits from deep thought and undivided attention.

- **Creative Projects:** For artists, writers, scientists, and thinkers with ADHD, hyperfocus can be the engine behind remarkable works. The ability to lose oneself in the creation process can lead to innovative ideas, breakthroughs, and the completion of substantial projects that might otherwise be daunting.

- **Spiritual Alignment:** For individuals with ADHD who also have a faith perspective, the dedication and passion seen in hyperfocus could be viewed as reflecting the guidance or inspiration of the Holy Spirit directing and enhancing one's gifts and talents.

- **Challenges and Management:** While hyperfocus can lead to significant achievements, it also poses challenges, such as neglecting other responsibilities or becoming so absorbed in one activity that transitioning to others becomes difficult. Learning to manage hyperfocus—leveraging its strengths while mitigating its downsides—is key for many with ADHD.

- **Relation to Flow State:** Hyperfocus shares similarities with the psychological concept of "flow" – a state of being completely involved in an activity for its own sake. Flow is characterized by a feeling of energized focus, full involvement, and enjoyment in the process. The main difference with hyperfocus associated with ADHD might be the difficulty in controlling when the state starts or ends.

Hyperfocus as a Gift

Viewing hyperfocus through the lens of the Holy Spirit who is believed to empower and guide, adds a rich layer of meaning to this trait. It can be seen as a divine tool that, when aligned with the Holy Spirit, enhances the ability to contribute uniquely and powerfully to the world. This perspective encourages a holistic view of ADHD, recognizing hyperfocus as a gift from God the Father through Jesus Christ.

In practical terms, individuals can foster an environment that maximizes the benefits of hyperfocus by setting up dedicated times and spaces for deep work, choosing projects aligned with their passions and talents, and using mindfulness or other strategies to gently transition in and out of hyperfocused states. Ultimately, whether viewed through a psychological, spiritual, or combined lens, hyperfocus is a testament to the human brain's incredible capacity for intense engagement and creativity. Its potential, particularly in those with ADHD, is a reminder of the diverse ways people can excel and contribute not only to society but also to the kingdom of God.

Family Creativity and Keeping My Interests

Growing up with ADHD in the school system of the 1980s and 1990s was somewhat challenging for me. The 1980s were great! Since technology had not yet surfaced with cell phones and the Internet, most of my activities involved playing outside or playing Nintendo games. Back then, I always seemed to be busy with something. However, my classroom interests were much different. In kindergarten and first grade, I remember being amazing at math. It was always something that engaged me. I think I owe that to my dad. He was my inspiration when it came to mathematics. In the early 1980s, my dad would draw up blueprints for houses. I was very young, and drafting was hard to understand, but it was always something that I loved to watch my dad do. He would show me the simple math and measurements that were involved in his projects.

Times had changed, and so had dad's career. He no longer did any drafting work—instead, I would only see Grandpa Hickenbottom perform drafting work for his own projects in our family's wood shop office at his house. Whenever I visited Grandpa, I realized that woodworking had become his main focus as well, a beloved hobby rather than just a job. His personal projects would sometimes require drafting, but I seldom saw him perform the drafts.

Likewise, although Dad continued drafting occasionally in the shop office, he too only engaged in this work at Grandpa's house, and never while I was around. His primary attention was devoted to woodworking, especially when he brought me along to the workshop. During those times, we would tackle various woodworking projects, sometimes for personal use, and occasionally for his employer. I cherished these moments deeply, as they provided me with a unique space to channel my creativity, a trait I've come to appreciate even more due to my ADHD.

The very best thing Grandpa and Dad did for me was to give me the space to be creative. Whether it was driving a nail into a board or helping Dad draw lines on his draft board, there was always something to build or make in the Hickenbottom family.

God demonstrates in the Old Testament His desire to give us creativity and craftmanship woven into our very being. In the story of Oholiab and Bezalel, God does just that.

"The Lord said to Moses, "See, I have called by name Bezalel the son of Uri, son of Hur, of the tribe of Judah, and I have filled him with the Spirit of God, with ability and intelligence, with knowledge and all craftmanship, to devise artistic designs, to work in gold, silver, and bronze, in cutting stones for setting and in carving wood, to work in every craft. And behold, I have appointed with him Oholiab, the son of Ahisamach, of the tribe of Dan. And I have given to all able men ability, that they may make all that I have commanded you: the table and its utensils, and the pure lampstand with all its utensils, and the altar of incense, and the altar of burnt offering with its utensils, and the basin and its stand, and the finely worked garments, the holy garments for Aaron the priest and the garments of his sons, for their service as priests, and the anointing oil and fragrant incense for the Holy Place. According to all that I have commanded you, they shall do."

Exodus 31:1-11

This story is so inspiring to me. God took two men and blessed them with creativity, knowledge, and wisdom. We must pass down our craftsmanship and creativity to others, specifically to our children. This honors God, and in doing so creates a positive interest in the mindset of someone who has ADHD, especially a young child. God still provides the same gifting as He did to

Bezalel and Oholiab. We learn by partnering with the Holy Spirit. Then we pass on our experiences, knowledge, and wisdom to our children or community. It is our responsibility as adults to honor our children and youth by teaching them these principles. For ADHD experiences to be successful and interesting, doing this is a must.

Understanding the influence of the Holy Spirit on creativity in individuals with ADHD reveals new possibilities for harnessing their unique abilities. This realization deepens your connection with the Holy Spirit and enhances your relationship with God the Father.

Key Takeaways

1. **Divine Inspiration through the Holy Spirit:** Highlight how the Holy Spirit acts as a profound source of inspiration, enabling individuals with ADHD to leverage their creative potential beyond ordinary limits.

2. **Biblical Basis for Creativity:** Discuss specific scriptures and teachings from Jesus that support the idea of creativity as a divine gift, particularly valuable in those with ADHD, showcasing how these traits are not just challenges but blessings that can lead to innovative thinking and problem-solving.

3. **Integration of Faith and Daily Life:** Encourage the practical application of biblical teachings and reliance on the Holy Spirit to manage daily life and enhance creativity. This integration helps in aligning one's life with spiritual values and maximizing personal talents.

Reflect on Your Creative Process

- **Identifying Creativity:** Think about a moment when you felt highly creative or productive. What were you doing? How did it feel physically and emotionally? Write down your thoughts.

- **The Holy Spirit's Influence:** Reflect on how you perceive the role of the Holy Spirit in your creative activities. Can you identify any specific instances when you felt guided or inspired in a way that you believe was influenced by the Holy Spirit? Journal these experiences.

Exercise - Divergent Thinking Practice

1. Choose a common object in your home—like a spoon, a pillow, or a shoe.
2. Set a timer for 5 minutes. List as many different uses for this object as you can think of, no matter how unconventional.

3. Review your list. Reflect on how this exercise might mirror the way your mind works in everyday situations, especially when tackling problems or challenges. Consider how the Holy Spirit might be inviting you to think outside the box in other areas of your life.

Hyperfocus Evaluation

1. Identify a recent project or activity where you experienced hyperfocus. Describe the project and your level of focus.

2. Analyze the impact of this hyperfocus. Did it have positive outcomes? Were there negative consequences, such as neglecting other responsibilities?

3. Pray for insight. Ask the Holy Spirit to help you harness this ability for hyperfocus while maintaining balance with other duties and relationships.

Prayer

Lord, thank You for the gift of creativity and the unique way my mind works with ADHD. I invite Your Holy Spirit to guide my thoughts and ideas, so they may reflect Your glory and bring innovation and solutions where they are needed. Help me to recognize Your influence in my creative processes and to use my gifts responsibly and joyfully. Amen.

CHAPTER THREE

JOURNEY TOWARD THE SPIRIT OF REJECTION

Chapter Three

Journey Toward the Spirit of Rejection

Medicated Self vs. Unmedicated Self

One of the most compelling topics I have covered so far in this book is the concept of having a medicated versus an unmedicated personality. When I first took Ritalin in third grade, a paradigm shift occurred in my brain. I was faced with the challenge of learning how to manage ADHD while medicated, as opposed to being unmedicated. I previously wrote that my medicated self grew up learning how to cope with ADHD in the way the world expected me to. In contrast, my unmedicated self was markedly different. It was almost as if I was reverting to my third-grade self as an adult. Today, I still take medication to assist with focus. However, I have learned to be a good steward of my mind, even when off the medication. All day long, I can operate just fine while on medication, but being off it requires an intense amount of self-awareness and a desire to master myself. I also partner with the Holy Spirit to lead and guide me in the areas where I cannot focus well when I am off the medication.

God desires an intimate relationship with us—a relationship that is tailored to fit who we are. In my adult life, I have found it difficult to connect well relationally with God the Father. For a long time, I looked at the Father as an authority figure who would keep me in line and get mad at me if I did wrong.

Jesus said, "If you have seen me, you have seen the Father." This means we live in complete fulfillment of the law (the Old Testament). Jesus loved people unconditionally and demonstrated this on multiple occasions throughout the Gospels.

With this being my worldview, I always thought something had to be fixed or that I needed to be a certain way. The truth is, the only true way I grow closer relationally with the Father is through the Holy Spirit. I partner with Him to learn how to manage ADHD when I am not medicated. This may sound strange to an unbeliever, but the experience is one that I can testify has changed my life. The more I seek guidance from the Holy Spirit on how to manage my thoughts, desires, peers, emotions and situations, the closer I grow relationally to the Father.

Effects of Medication

In my adult life, my routine starts in the kitchen each morning where I take two key medications: Ritalin and Concerta. Concerta provides a steady, 12-hour release of stimulants, which ensures a consistent level of focus throughout the day. Yet, I found myself needing a bit more, so my doctor and I decided to supplement this with a four-hour Ritalin dose for an additional morning boost.

Time	Medication	Dosage	Effect
Morning	Ritalin	10 mg	Short-term boost of focus for 4 hours
Throughout the day	Concerta	54 mg	Long-lasting, steady focus for 12 hours

Ritalin begins to work about 20-25 minutes after taking it, ushering in a profound state of hyperfocus that feels like a shift in mental state. This boost is similar to the effect of a morning coffee, which I avoid because I'm already on prescribed stimulants.

Adjusting the Ritalin dose is critical—it must be precisely calibrated as both an overdose and underdose can significantly alter its impact. This balance is a frequent topic of discussion with my doctor. Concerta, on the other hand, has been consistently effective and is among the better treatments available to me.

Feature	Ritalin	Concerta
Drug Type	Immediate-release stimulant	Extended-release stimulant
Onset of Action	20-30 minutes	1 hour
Duration	3-4 hours per dose	10-12 hours
Dosage Forms	Tablets (5 mg, 10 mg, 20 mg)	Extended-release tablets (18 mg, 27 mg, 36 mg, 54 mg)
Common Uses	Managing ADHD symptoms, narcolepsy	Long-term management of ADHD symptoms
Side Effects	Insomnia, nervousness, increased heart rate	Reduced appetite, sleep issues, headache
Benefits	Quick symptom control, flexibility in timing	Consistent symptom control throughout the day
Patient Feedback	Effective for short-term focus, requires multiple doses	Preferred for all-day coverage, once daily dosing
Personal Experience	Good for targeted focus, like meetings or specific tasks	Helps maintain a steady focus throughout the day; less worry about re-dosing

Entering hyperfocus not only heightens my mental clarity but also physically energizes me. Skillfully managing this focused state, particularly transitioning between tasks, is crucial. While medications help facilitate this, achieving deep focus isn't exclusively reliant on them.

Having been on Ritalin since the age of nine, and now at 43, I notice profound differences when I am unmedicated. My emotional state often dictates whether I medicate, especially based on my anticipated daily activities. For less mentally demanding tasks, like cleaning the garage or working on my car, I might choose not to medicate.

On more cognitively intensive days, I use strategies such as jotting down tasks on a notepad or setting up reminders on my smart devices. These aids may seem excessive to some, but they are vital for maintaining focus because of my ADHD.

When not medicated, I find it more effective to listen rather than speak, particularly in group settings. This approach requires discipline, which I derive from my faith. I often turn to the Holy Spirit for support in managing impulsivity and maintaining focus.

Whether medicated or not, it is essential to manage how I interact with others and control my mood. An unexpected interruption can disrupt my hyperfocus, leading to irritation, which might come across as rudeness to others. Over time, I have learned to manage these challenges better.

Overall, medication has been a crucial component of my strategy for managing ADHD, helping me to function optimally while also encouraging me to develop coping mechanisms that are effective with or without medication.

Parable of the Sower and Soils

In Mark Chapter 4, Jesus talks about a seed and the Sower. I want to break this down slowly and connect this example to ADHD and being unmedicated.

Mark 4:1-12

1. Again he began to teach beside the sea. And a very large crowd gathered about him, so that he got into a boat and sat in it on the sea, and the whole crowd was beside the sea on the land.

2. And he was teaching them many things in parables, and in his teaching he said to them:

3. "Listen! Behold, a sower went out to sow.

4. And as he sowed, some seed fell along the path, and the birds came and devoured it.

5. Other seed fell on rocky ground, where it did not have much soil, and immediately it sprang up, since it had no depth of soil.

6. And when the sun rose, it was scorched, and since it had no root, it withered away.

7. Other seed fell among thorns, and the thorns grew up and choked it, and it yielded no grain.

8. And other seeds fell into good soil and produced grain, growing up and increasing and yielding thirtyfold and sixtyfold and a hundredfold."

9. And he said, "He who has ears to hear, let him hear."

10. And when he was alone, those around him with the twelve asked him about the parables.

11. And he said to them, "To you has been given the secret of the kingdom of God, but for those outside everything is in parables,

12. so that 'they may indeed see but not perceive, and may indeed hear but not understand, lest they should turn and be forgiven.'"

I want to start with verse 5: "Other seed fell on rocky ground, where it did not have much soil, and immediately it sprang up, since it had no depth of soil." Relating this to ADHD, my unmedicated mind immediately identifies with the seed falling on the rocky ground. With ADHD, I have a lot of energy and quickly get excited about new things. The seed springs up because it had no depth of soil. What I mean is that I start things quickly and then lose interest just as fast. I sprout something new, then leave it alone or lose interest. In verse 6, the sun comes up, and the seed is scorched.

Why is this important? In my experience, the world views ADHD this way. The phrase "LOOK, SQUIRREL!" comes to mind. I admit that when unmedicated, I can become intellectually lazy and just sprout one seed, then burn up, and move on to the next. Not managing your mind well and partnering with the Holy Spirit to grow while unmedicated will always keep you in this cycle.

On the flip side, medication does help fix this issue. Think of it this way: some might say, "I need coffee to wake up and start my morning." A person with ADHD, on the other hand, might say, "Let me take some medication so I can focus and not grow on rocky soil." This creates a dependency, making me feel like I need the medication in order to do well. If that were true, I wouldn't be created well in the image of God. Medication is great, and I admit I use it. But medication only works for most situations. In my experience, if you don't manage your mind properly and grow relationally with the Father through the Holy Spirit, ADHD will always be a seed that burns up and yields no fruit. For me, having ADHD and taking medication means I see it as "I can live without it." Suffice it to say, I work more interdependently with medication. It does its part, and I do mine. Medication makes it easier for me to function during a professional workday. But just like that cup of coffee in the morning, I can live without it too.

If I had a dependent mindset, I would probably be worried about the ADHD medication shortage we experienced in 2022-2023. I would think things like, "I will mess up at work and not get my job done!" or "I will annoy others and not fit in socially!" Do you see the identity issues of dependency on ADHD medication? Instead, I think, "I will need extra sleep tonight because I won't have medication tomorrow." or "I will have to listen to the Holy Spirit and understand when He says, 'JUST BE SILENT!' in that meeting with my boss."

I know my identity in Jesus Christ, so "How will others think of me?" is not a concern. If they waste their mental energy on such things, that is their personal issue, not mine.

Now let's connect all this by looking at what Jesus says when He explains the parable to His disciples.

Mark 4:15-17

1. And these are the ones along the path, where the word is sown: when they hear, Satan immediately comes and takes away the word that is sown in them.

2. And these are the ones sown on rocky ground: the ones who, when they hear the word, immediately receive it with joy.

3. And they have no root in themselves, but endure for a while; then, when tribulation or persecution arises on account of the word, immediately they fall away.

Verse 17 explains it best: "They have no root in themselves." Sound familiar? Sure, it does. I just connected the idea that an ADHD mind not pursuing relational growth with the Father through the Holy Spirit will never bear fruit. It will just be that seed that burns up because it has no firm root in itself or its identity in Jesus Christ. The last part Jesus says here is, "when tribulation or persecution arises on account of the word, immediately they fall away." Jesus is talking about getting excited about the word of God and then running away when things get tough. This is true in what I am saying as well. In an unmedicated ADHD mindset, I am the person who gets excited about something, engages for a bit, and then falls away. When things get tough, I have no firm foundation to stand my ground and will ultimately fall away, as Jesus says. I will conform to a fear mindset of "I need my medication," or "What do people think of me when I am annoying because I am off my medication?"

The lessons drawn from the Parable of the Sower illustrate how quickly one can fall away when challenges arise, much like the struggles experienced with ADHD when lacking a firm foundation. This understanding of fleeting enthusiasm and shallow roots sets the stage to explore deeper relational dynamics, particularly the influences that shaped early perceptions of rejection.

Laying the Foundation for the Spirit of Rejection

During my fifth-grade year, I was tested and placed in special education classes. This was a difficult experience for a young fifth grader trying to establish an identity among his peers. Being labeled as the "Special Ed Kid" completely wrecked my social identity. Despite this, I still tried to hang out with the popular crowd. However, this only led to a false identity of who I thought I needed to be. For the first time in my life, I started hating my ADHD and blaming it for my inability to fit in.

Struggling to fit in socially, I would rely on my medication during the day just to get by. By the time the bell rang, my dosage of Ritalin had worn off, and I would revert to the unmedicated version of myself. This created a stark contrast in my personality, making it even harder to fit in. I felt like I was living a double life, one where I was medicated and could function somewhat normally, and another where I was the hyperactive, inattentive kid who couldn't keep up.

Despite these challenges, my life was becoming busier. In fifth grade, I started playing the saxophone. Music was a wonderful outlet for expressing my loud personality. Additionally, I participated in a fifth-grade basketball program. This gave me a sense of belonging and achievement. Sports, including baseball, basketball and football, played a significant role in my life during fifth and sixth grade. Keeping myself busy was a way to feel more in control and successful.

However, my classroom life was a different story. I struggled academically, especially in social studies. Social studies interested me, but my grades didn't reflect my enthusiasm. It was frustrating to be passionate about a subject but not see that passion translate into good grades.

As a result, I had reached a point where I needed to start taking notes. As a fifth-grade boy with ADHD, the idea of taking notes seemed daunting. I was easily distracted and couldn't grasp how to take effective notes. For instance, while I enjoyed skimming through textbooks to learn about different periods of history, listening to lectures bored me. The disconnect between my interests and my academic performance only deepened my sense of rejection and frustration.

Looking back, it's clear that these experiences laid the foundation for a spirit of rejection that would follow me for years. The social and academic struggles I faced in fifth grade were just the beginning of a long journey of self-discovery and acceptance.

The Sixth Grade and New Challenges

The year was 1992, and I was in sixth grade. This year was challenging for me as well. My homeroom teacher was that "old school" strict teacher that everyone hoped they would never get. But in all fairness, this was what I needed. Despite being an older lady, she could keep up with my hyperactive energy. Many would say, "You have THAT teacher." It was no secret that she was tough, but her discipline helped me in ways I didn't realize at the time.

In addition to the challenges at school, a few other significant events happened to me that year. My first cousin, who was the same age as me and was more like a close brother, moved away. My neighbor, who was my best friend, also moved away. Furthermore, my brother was now a senior in high school and would be joining the Army National Guard after graduating. That year, it felt like everyone was abandoning me, and I struggled to cope with these changes.

Looking back, grade school boiled down to three adverse experiences: first, I dealt with initial inspiration that gradually faded; second, my self-worth declined significantly; and third, rejection set in, deeply affecting my identity. These experiences laid the groundwork for the challenges I would face in the years to come, shaping my journey of self-discovery and resilience.

The Downward Spiral Towards Rejection

I would like to illustrate how this downward spiral led me to a spirit of rejection.

- Not being inspired to learn academics simply meant I did not care to do the schoolwork.

- I just wanted to fit in and to have people like me.

- I began to see myself rejected by my friends and social cliques as I was labeled the "The Special ED Kid."

These are very critical points in my early adolescent years. The fact that I was not inspired led to no motivation. Then, wanting to fit in led to opening the door to the spirit of rejection. Finally, feeling rejected and having to prove myself, I found the need to adopt a false identity for myself.

These early experiences set the stage for my ongoing struggles with self-worth and acceptance. It wasn't until much later in life that I discovered a path to healing and understanding, and this path was deeply rooted in the Holy Trinity.

Teach the Holy Trinity to the Next Generation

Right from the start, it is important for young minds to grasp the profound truths of the Holy Trinity—God the Father, Jesus Christ, and the Holy Spirit. Understanding that God the Father is the foundation of all relationships is crucial—you belong to Him, wholly and completely. This foundational knowledge sets the stage for everything else in your spiritual journey.

Now, let's turn the dial... Jesus Christ represents your identity. Striving to be like Jesus isn't just a goal; it's a transformative realization that begins the moment you dedicate your life to Jesus Christ. Throughout my journey with ADHD, which spans over 38 years of both struggles and revelations, I've come to appreciate just how essential this realization is. For too long, I didn't see that God the Father was always there, arms wide open, ready to confirm my place in His grand family. Missing this connection led me down paths filled with shadows of shame, where I constantly felt inadequate—precisely what Satan wants us to believe.

I've mentioned before that Satan has his schemes. He tries to imprison those with ADHD, persecuting them for their unique minds and casting a false identity over them for the world to see. Why? Because he fears the ADHD mindset. He is terrified of what you might become if you fully dedicate your life to Jesus Christ, live like Him, and harness the transformative power the Holy Spirit brings.

Turn the dial once more... the Holy Spirit is your destiny, calling you to action. The Spirit urges you to DO, to step into the roles you were created for. That's the final twist that brings everything full circle.

Teaching the Trinity in Everyday Life

If you are mentoring young ones or simply enriching your own understanding, integrating the reality of the Holy Trinity into daily life is vital:

Belonging - God the Father: Ensure that children or those new to faith understand they are an integral part of God's family. Highlight scriptures that demonstrate God's unwavering love and His joyful affirmation of each individual as His beloved child. This firm foundation inspires confidence to explore one's true identity.

Identity - Jesus Christ: Dive into the Gospels together. Show how Jesus reached out to those who were marginalized or misunderstood. His unconditional acceptance is a powerful affirmation of individual worth and provides a model for how to embrace one's identity. Through Jesus, you can see yourself not as the world labels you, but as God sees you—perfectly made and deeply loved.

Destiny - The Holy Spirit: Foster a dynamic relationship with the Holy Spirit, the divine guide who propels you into action and equips you to fulfill your God-given destiny. Practices such as prayer, meditating on Bible passages, and keeping a journal of spiritual insights are excellent ways to strengthen this connection.

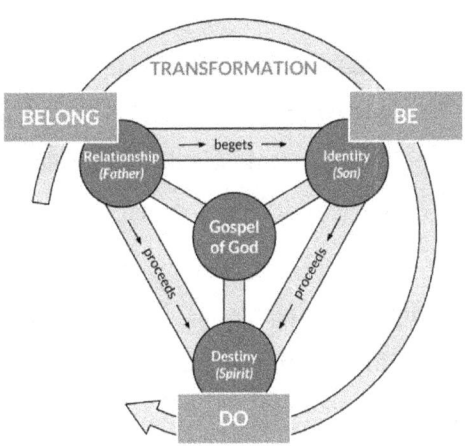

By grounding these teachings in a personal, deep relationship with the Holy Trinity, you are provided with a spiritual roadmap that's not only scripturally sound but deeply transformative. This approach isn't just about understanding theological concepts; it's about living out a faith that navigates real-life challenges—starting with belonging, moving through identity, and ultimately achieving your destiny with the guidance of the Holy Spirit. This comprehensive method is especially crucial for navigating life's complexities, whether you have ADHD or not, with the grace and strength that only comes from Jesus Christ.

Transitioning from the exploration of the transformative power of the Holy Trinity, it's vital to internalize the concepts of belonging, identity, and destiny. Delving deep into the Holy Spirit's role in guiding toward your God-given purpose can give you the strength and confidence to live out your faith authentically.

Key Takeaways

1. **Understanding the Medicated vs. Unmedicated Self:** Reflect on the journey of managing ADHD with and without medication, emphasizing the importance of self-awareness and partnership with the Holy Spirit for holistic growth and management.

2. **Effects of Medication:** Summarize the impact of medication on focus and productivity, highlighting the need for balance and precision in dosage management.

3. **Parable of the Sower and ADHD:** Connect the struggles of an unmedicated ADHD mind with the imagery of the seed falling on rocky ground in Jesus' parable, emphasizing the importance of cultivating a firm foundation through spiritual growth.

4. **Laying the Foundation for Rejection:** Explore how early experiences of academic struggles, social rejection, and identity challenges laid the groundwork for a spirit of rejection, setting the stage for ongoing struggles with self-worth and acceptance.

5. **Teaching the Holy Trinity:** Emphasize the importance of understanding the Holy Trinity in everyday life, highlighting belonging to God the Father, identity in Jesus Christ, and destiny guided by the Holy Spirit as foundational principles for spiritual growth and resilience.

6. **Practical Integration:** Encourage the integration of these teachings into daily life, emphasizing practices such as prayer, meditation on

Scripture, and journaling to deepen one's relationship with the Holy Trinity and navigate life's challenges with grace and strength.

Memory Lane Exercise

- Draw a timeline of your life journey, focusing on moments related to your experiences with ADHD, medication, and spirituality. Mark key events, both positive and negative, that have shaped your understanding of yourself and your relationship with God.

Reflective Questions

- Reflect on a moment when you felt the presence of the Holy Spirit guiding you in managing your ADHD or navigating challenges related to medication. How did this experience impact your faith and spiritual growth?

- Identify a challenging situation where you struggled with rejection or self-worth. How did you overcome this obstacle, and what role did your faith play in providing strength and resilience?

Role-Playing Scenarios

- Imagine you are in a conversation with a friend or family member who doesn't understand ADHD or the challenges it presents. Practice explaining your experiences and the role of medication in managing ADHD. Reflect on how this conversation might deepen understanding and foster empathy in your relationships.

Interactive Journal

- Write a letter to yourself during a challenging moment in your journey with ADHD and medication. Offer words of encouragement, reassurance, and hope based on your current understanding and experiences with faith and spirituality.

- Describe a time you engaged in scripture and prayer and listening to the Holy Spirit. Explain how this method helped you cope with the challenges of ADHD and medication. Reflect on how this practice has contributed to your overall well-being and sense of connection with the Holy Trinity.

Prayer

- Begin by expressing gratitude for the lessons learned and the growth experienced on your spiritual journey.

- Reflect on moments of forgiveness, both for yourself and others, and ask for peace and healing in any areas of lingering pain or resentment. Pray for continued growth, understanding, and strength as you walk in faith and partnership with the Holy Trinity.

CHAPTER FOUR

BATTLING ISOLATION

AND IDENTITY

Chapter Four

Battling Isolation and Identity

Entering 7th Grade

The summer came to a close, and it was time to prepare for junior high. Seventh grade would prove to be another academically difficult year for me. Up until then, my learning disability classes—what I called LD classes—were a manageable part of my week. In fifth and sixth grade, I went a couple times each week, usually at the end of the day. It was a helpful routine, and I didn't feel isolated from the rest of the students. But when I got to seventh grade, everything changed. I suddenly felt as if I was on an island.

In junior high, we had a homeroom class. But for me, my homeroom was with the special education class. Being separated from the other students did not sit well with me at all. What if other students found out I had a learning disability (which was actually a result of ADHD)? The fear of rejection was all I could think about, and this terrified me! The shame was now turning into anger and rage. Trying to establish a reputable identity in seventh grade was hard enough, and now a special education class for homeroom? It was painful to know that I could do nothing to change this. So, I did the only thing I knew how to do: I would fight the system and rebel. My parents and educators were trying to help me academically, but I did not see it that way. I was more concerned about fitting in and being accepted.

To make matters worse, I was taken out of regular English classes and given what felt like busywork—a basic, black workbook with exercises that seemed like a joke. The questions were so simple that I couldn't help but feel insulted. I knew I could do better, but it was hard to care when the work didn't challenge me at all. After a while, I just stopped trying, which backfired because the teachers thought I wasn't getting it, or worse, that I was slacking off. The truth was, I just wanted to be in a regular class with my friends, learning things that mattered.

Math used to be my favorite subject. I was really into it until I got to seventh grade and had a teacher who seemed to have no interest in teaching me. My mom said she had her favorites, and I could see it. The kids who got good grades were the ones she paid attention to. I was there, trying to understand, but she wouldn't give me the time of day. It was like she had already decided I wasn't worth her effort. It hurt because I knew I could do math—I just needed someone to believe in me.

Things didn't get much better in eighth grade. I kept pushing back, insisting I could handle regular classes, and they finally let me into a regular English class. I was excited because it felt like a step toward what I wanted. I was actually good at public speaking, so when I gave my first presentation, I thought I nailed it. But I got a D. My mom and I had worked on a chicken feeder filled with M&Ms for my project. We painted it, made it look amazing, and I gave a great presentation. I was proud of it. But then I got that D, and it felt like a slap in the face. There was no explanation, no feedback—just a D. I couldn't help but think it was because the teacher didn't like me. It was demoralizing, especially since I had put so much effort into it.

The only class that felt like a safe space was science. My science teacher was different from the others. I felt like he actually cared. He would ask me what I needed and make sure I was okay. I found out later he was a friend of my family, but at the time, I just thought he was a good teacher. We built rockets, did lab experiments, and he made learning fun. I remember building my rocket, sanding the wings for aerodynamics, and feeling proud of what I was doing. When it launched, it didn't go as high as I hoped, but it didn't crash either. It was a small victory in a year full of struggles, and it felt good to have someone believe in me.

By the end of junior high, I was exhausted from being labeled the "special ed" kid. It was a tag that didn't fit me, but I couldn't shake it. I just wanted to be creative, to learn, and be with my friends. But when you are constantly pushed to the side, it's hard to feel like you belong. Those years were a mix of highs and lows, and the lows always came from feeling misunderstood and excluded. I wish there had been more teachers like my science teacher—people who saw my potential and didn't define me by a label. Those were the moments that made a difference, but they were too few and far between.

Football and Restless Leg Syndrome (RLS)

The fall of 1993, my seventh-grade year, was a transformative time for me as I tackled a new challenge: playing tackle football. Football had always held a special place in my heart, especially after winning a city championship in flag football during fifth grade. With each passing year, I felt myself getting faster and more skilled. However, as I prepared to play against older and larger opponents in seventh grade, a wave of fear washed over me.

As the football season kicked off, I noticed an overwhelming sense of fatigue engulfing me. I confided in my mom about how tired I felt all the time, but she attributed my exhaustion to the demands of being an athlete. However, the pain in my legs and the difficulty of getting out of bed in the mornings told a different story.

Navigating through the tumultuous waters of junior high, dealing with hormones, ADHD, and mood swings made it even harder for me to manage my anger. Seeking answers, my parents took me back to my ADHD doctor at Carle Hospital. During this visit, a possible correlation between my restless leg syndrome (RLS) and my ADHD in adolescence was discussed. In order to better understand my sleep issues, I underwent a sleep study, a process that involved being hooked up to numerous wires and sensors that would record my movements while I slept. Despite my initial concerns about falling asleep with all that equipment, I eventually managed to doze off.

The results of the sleep study were eye-opening. They revealed that my RLS was drastically impacting my sleep, academic performance, and sports abilities. As a teenager going through a growth spurt, my body needed sufficient rest to replenish itself. Armed with this newfound knowledge, I embarked on a journey to treat my restless leg syndrome and regain control over my academic and athletic pursuits.

Before starting medication for my RLS, I often had a really bad attitude, especially in the mornings. It wasn't just typical teenage moodiness—it was more like anger and frustration that made me hard to be around. To find out what was causing my outbursts, my mom decided to record me without my knowledge. She placed a tape recorder in the bathroom, the best place to capture my morning rants.

The next morning, after recording me, she played the tape for me. "Listen to yourself," she said, sounding worried. "You get so angry, yelling at me and being mean." When I heard my voice on the tape, I was shocked. It was like listening to a different person. The things I said were harsh, filled with anger and disrespect. "Is that really me?" I thought, stunned by my own behavior. It was a real eye-opener and made me realize I had a problem.

After hearing the tape, my mom and I decided to talk to my ADHD doctor. He said that my behavior might be connected to RLS, which can not only cause sleep problems but also lead to mood swings. With the new diagnosis, we went to the pharmacy to get my medication. The pharmacist looked at us strangely when we gave him the prescription, which was usually for Parkinson's disease. We told him it was also used to treat RLS, and his confused expression was rather entertaining since he had no idea what RLS was.

That first night after taking the medication, I slept like a baby. I felt rested for the first time in a long time. The next morning, my mother couldn't even wake me up. After adjusting my dosage a bit, waking up got easier. The sleep medication adjusted my serotonin levels and allowed me to get the proper amount of REM sleep. It took a little time to get the dosage right, but once we figured it out, my mood improved considerably. I wasn't as angry or irritable, and my mom was relieved to see the change in me. The medication also helped with the mood swings I would get when my ADHD medication wore off.

Taking medication for RLS made a big difference in my life. I could sleep better, which helped me feel more in control of my emotions. The anger and hostility that used to define my mornings became much less frequent. I was still a teenager with all the typical ups and downs, but at least now I could handle them without losing control. The medication was a turning point, helping me get back on track and find some stability in my life.

The Basketball Team

Now it was late fall 1993, and the seventh-grade basketball coach pulled me aside one morning. He said, "I would like you to try out for the team." You see, I was 6' 1" in seventh grade. I was a twig, but tall enough to be scouted by the coach. I took him up on the offer and tried out for the team. However, my grades were not the best since I had nothing to inspire me to learn. Not performing well with academics caused me to be cut from the basketball team. I remember the coach saying, "You made the team, but you are on the 'D' list for academics." In other words, having bad grades from the start meant an automatic cut from the team. Receiving the news that I did not make the team was tough for me to hear. I kept asking myself, "Why would a coach ask me to try out and then cut me from his team?"

The fact I did not make the team was now common knowledge among my peers. Going to school felt horrible. I remember walking into school in the morning and sitting down on the bleachers with my friends. Fear started to build up. What were my peers going to think of me for not making the basketball team? More importantly, what were the girls going to think? I had pretty much labeled myself as a loser because I didn't make the basketball team.

I was walking home one day with one of my good friends when a question arose amid our everyday conversation. He asked, "Why didn't you make the team?" I glanced over, and then I looked him in the eye. Then shame and guilt just poured over me. I looked like a deer staring into headlights. He proceeded to ask me again, "Why didn't you make the team?" At that moment, I tried to come up with a good explanation that would mask my shame of getting bad grades—hiding the fact that I had ADHD and was in special education classes. "I don't know why," I replied softly. The guilt and shame now attached itself to a lie. I knew the reason. I was just ashamed to reveal the true answer.

Most of the popular boys wanted to be on the basketball team. To be a part of the basketball team meant I was in with the popular crowd. Basketball was the one sport that defined popularity in seventh and eighth grade junior high. I was trying very hard to be accepted by popular social cliques. I wanted to fit in and for people to like me. Looking back on this now, I finally understand what happened to me during that time in my life.

The Basketball Checklist

Let's look back at the transformation model earlier in Chapter Two. I will correlate all three sections to a checklist I made for my heroic identity of being on the basketball team.

DO: Perform well and make the basketball team.

BE: Making the basketball team meant I would be good enough to be accepted among my peers and popular social cliques.

BELONG: Being accepted by the popular social cliques meant that I would belong with the popular crowd.

At this point, you should be able to identify the problem. The cycle transformation direction was backward. In other words, I was going the wrong direction in correlation to the transformation model. Furthermore, let's break things down after being rejected by not making the basketball team and still going the wrong way in the model.

DO: I was trying to perform well to be on the basketball team and I did not make it.

BE: Since I did not make the basketball team I could not fit in with the popular crowd, which made me feel disqualified for popularity among my peers.

BELONG: Unable to prove that I could be popular created a reality for me that I could not belong. I started to blame ADHD for not performing well.

As you can see, it was at this exact moment in my life where I started a downward spiral of problems—going the wrong way in the transformation model that was referenced in Chapter 3. I began to allow so many things into my life—evil things. If I had just gone the other direction like the transformation model shows, I would have been in a different situation. Let me put that in a checklist.

- ✓ Anger
- ✓ Shame
- ✓ Guilt

✓ Rejection

Imagine how this situation would affect me as an adult. Anger, shame, guilt, and rejection left unchecked will just continue to grow. I opened doors for the enemy (Satan) to attack me in these areas of my life. Everything from the way I treated people to how I would behave in certain situations showed a direct correlation in Satan using these areas to disrupt my life and cause me to behave in a way that was unacceptable. All would result around this checklist.

<u>Look even deeper at the transformation model:</u>

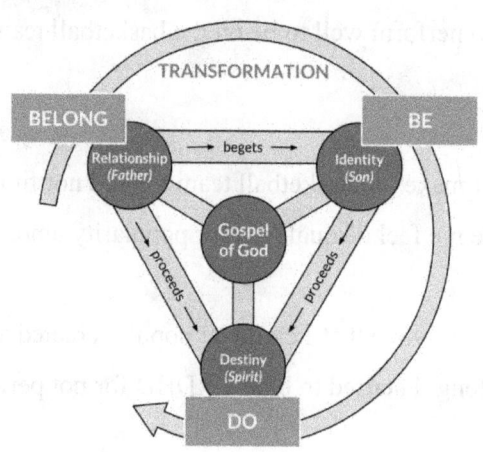

You see that the "BELONG" part is the "Father God" in the Holy Trinity. It should have started with a relationship with God, the Father—not performing to be a part of something. My identity (which is the "BE" part of the transformation model and the "Son" part of the Holy Trinity) was inverted. Not to mention, I was going against my identity through Jesus Christ. Ultimately, 20+ years later, as an adult, I am cleaning up the mess. This very act shaped my identity, and it all started in junior high.

As I conquered each day with the help of my new medication for RLS, I found myself grappling with more than just the physical symptoms. My spirit, too, was restless. Junior high was drawing to a close, and with it came the realization that while I could medicate my body, the struggle for acceptance and understanding within myself was a different battle entirely. The difficulties I faced in finding my place and proving my worth were not just challenges to overcome but were shaping who I was becoming.

Junior high had its ups and downs—more downs, if I'm honest. The constant struggle with ADHD and the labels from being in special education classes wore me down. Yet, there were glimpses of hope, like my science teacher who believed in me, or the moments on the football field that gave me a break from the constant judgment. But as junior high drew to a close, I couldn't shake the feeling that I was still being held back by something I couldn't control.

The pressure to fit in, the struggle with grades, and the search for a place where I truly belonged were relentless. The hits kept coming, and every time I thought I was getting ahead, something else would remind me of my limitations. The rejection from the basketball team because of my grades and the growing distance from my friends felt like evidence that the system was against me. I just wanted a chance to prove myself, to show I wasn't just "the special ed kid" everyone thought I was.

Key Takeaways

1. **Navigating Junior High with ADHD:** This chapter explored the complexities of living with ADHD during junior high, from academic challenges to the emotional turmoil of being placed in a special education class. The struggle to find acceptance and normalcy in a world that often feels unforgiving is a central theme.

2. **Physical and Mental Health Challenges:** The discovery of Restless Leg Syndrome (RLS) added an additional layer of difficulty. Managing this condition required medical intervention, revealing the broader impact of physical health on mental well-being and academic performance.

3. **Sports as an Outlet and Pressure Point:** Football and basketball were not only activities but also a means to connect with peers. The rejection from the basketball team due to academic issues served as a catalyst for deeper feelings of inadequacy and shame.

4. **Family Support and Emotional Awareness:** The tape-recorded message from my mother was a wake-up call, emphasizing the importance of family support in addressing behavioral issues. It highlighted the role of anger and its potential impact on relationships, suggesting a need for emotional awareness and growth.

5. **Resilience and the Search for Identity:** Throughout the chapter, there was a sense of resilience despite setbacks. This resilience set the stage for a broader exploration of identity.

Memory Lane Exercise

- Draw a timeline of your junior high years. Mark key events, both positive and negative, that shaped your understanding of yourself and your ADHD.

Reflective Questions

- What was one of the most challenging moments during these years, and how did you handle it?
- Identify a positive memory from this period and describe how it has impacted your life.

Role-Playing Scenarios

Imagine you're back in junior high. You face a situation where you must explain your ADHD to a friend or teacher who doesn't understand it.

- Write out what you would say.

- Reflect on how this might have changed the trajectory of your junior high experience. Discuss or journal about the potential impacts.

Interactive Journal

- Describe a teacher from junior high who influenced you (positively or negatively). What would you say to them now, knowing what you do about yourself and ADHD?

- Write about a hobby or interest you had during junior high. How did this activity help you cope with or distract from your challenges?

Prayer

- Begin by expressing gratitude for the lessons learned and strengths gained during your junior high years.

- Move into a time of forgiveness, asking for peace regarding any negative experiences or relationships from that time.

- Pray for those who might still be struggling from their own junior high experiences, that they might find healing and understanding.

CHAPTER FIVE

IDENTIFY CRISIS

Chapter Five

Identity Crisis

The Conference Room

As eighth grade progressed, my anxiety grew. Teachers began pulling me aside more often, each with their own idea of how to "fix" me. I started to question whether there was something fundamentally wrong with me. The worst moment came when I was called into a conference room, filled with all my teachers. My mother was there too, which only added to the sense of foreboding. I felt like a defendant on trial, with no defense and no idea what I'd done wrong.

The meeting started with a barrage of criticisms—my disruptive behavior, my lack of interest in academics, and my refusal to conform. Every word felt like a blow, and all I could do was sit there and take it. I wanted to speak up, to explain that I wasn't trying to be difficult, but it felt like they'd already made up their minds. My LD (learning disability) teacher started talking first. I knew I was in trouble, but it was hard to focus on what she said because all I felt was apprehension. My mother sat there silently while I tried to hold back tears.

The only ones who seemed to believe in me were my science teacher and my mother. My science teacher, a family friend, spoke up to defend me: "You're a brilliant young man with a lot of potential," he said. My mother remained silent but supportive, her presence providing a comforting anchor amid the storm of criticism. Even with their belief in me, it couldn't change the overall perception that I was a problem that needed to be solved.

Sitting in that conference room, I felt more like an object than a person. The real issue wasn't just my behavior—it was the relentless pressure to be someone I wasn't. The teachers wanted me to fit into their mold, but I just wanted to be myself. The meeting ended without a clear resolution, leaving only a vague sense of unease about what was coming next. It felt like junior high was determined to squeeze the life out of me, and I wasn't sure I had the strength to keep fighting.

As I reflected on the harsh words and misunderstandings, it became clear that traditional methods weren't reaching me. This realization sparked my journey toward understanding how inspiration plays a critical role in education, especially for those who learn differently.

Junior High's Lasting Impact

Junior high was coming to a close, and my ADHD situation hadn't improved. As I transitioned into a full teenage boy, I started experiencing even more anxiety and pressure to be someone I was not. Teachers continued pulling me aside, trying to "fix" me. I constantly asked myself, "Am I broken?"

I couldn't forget that day in the conference room. Surrounded by all my teachers and my mom, I sat with fear and anxiety, not knowing what to expect. As they addressed my disruptive behavior and lack of interest in academics, they told me, "You need to fix all of this." Even though my science teacher, my one true ally, reiterated his belief in my potential, I still felt alone in that room.

After the school year ended and summer began, the anxiety and dread from junior high lingered, leaving me uncertain about how I'd manage high school. But I knew one thing for sure: being treated like a problem to be fixed wasn't going to help me succeed. That meeting became a turning point, shaping my understanding of the importance of inspiration and empathy in education.

Finding My Voice

As the teachers seemed to throw all my failures at me, I started to get defensive, like a dog backed into a corner. The more they pressed me, the more I wanted to fight back. No one seemed interested in hearing my side of the story, even though they kept asking me what my problem was and how they could help me. I just wanted them to understand my pain—that I am who I am, and I don't want to be the person they expect me to be.

Looking back, I can see that most of my teachers were genuinely trying to help, but I didn't fit into the traditional learning system. I didn't care about their rules or standards. I just wanted to be accepted for who I was. It's clear that some teachers were doing their best, but others seemed more focused on their own interests. My science teacher was different, though. He made learning fun and believed in me. (When I became a teacher later in my life, he was the inspiration behind some of the fun activities I did with my students.)

Finding Inspiration

I realized that I needed inspiration to learn. Without it, I felt disconnected, like I was just going through the motions in class, not really absorbing anything. This was especially true for ADHD kids like me; our minds raced a mile a minute, and the traditional sit-still-and-listen approach didn't work. I needed something more—something that would catch my attention and make me want to learn.

Inspiration for me came from teachers who made learning an experience. It wasn't about memorizing facts or filling in worksheets; it was about engaging my curiosity and encouraging my creativity. My science teacher let us do hands-on experiments, build models, and launch rockets. Learning became fun, not a chore. It was the moments of connection with teachers who believed in me that helped me see education as an opportunity.

Another source of inspiration was relevance in what I was learning. If I could connect what I was studying to something meaningful in my life, I was much more likely to stay engaged. It wasn't just about getting through the curriculum—it was about finding a personal connection to the material. When learning felt relevant, I was drawn in, and I actually wanted to be in class.

Being Who I Was Created to Be

One thing I've learned over the years is that many people try to persuade me to be someone I'm not. Some do it with good intentions; others are driven by their own selfish motives. Sometimes it's to make their lives easier, to fit their narrative, or because they think they know what's best for me. Too many times, people looked at my ADHD as something to "fix," as if it were a problem to be solved. But when I read Proverbs 19:21, I knew that God created me with ADHD, and it wasn't something to be fixed—it was a gift. It was my responsibility to be a good steward of my unique mind, to find ways to use it for good.

Knowing what I know now, these are some things I wish I would have done differently in that conference room:

- **Take notes instead of just listening:** Writing down their concerns would have shown I cared enough to remember what they said.

- **Hold myself accountable:** When someone spoke to me directly, I should have understood that it wasn't personal, just feedback in a professional capacity.

- **Understand that I am who I am in Christ, and not what they want me to be:** I could acknowledge their advice but also know that my identity is rooted elsewhere.

- **Apologize and repent:** Some examples they gave were moments when I knew I needed to behave better, and ADHD wasn't an excuse.

It would have been hard to act or think this way as a 12- to 14-year-old in junior high. At that age, I did not have the life experiences to understand the four points I just made. If you're the parent of a child with ADHD, I would encourage you to challenge and inspire them to try to understand these values. But understanding them will not be an immediate fix. Rather, it will take diligence on your part. Then you will take joy in watching your child grow into these values.

Encouragement for Parents

I would like to encourage you as a parent who may be very anxious about your child with ADHD, and the situations that may occur. In the book of Matthew, Chapter 6, Jesus gives us the cure for anxiety. Verse 33 states, "But seek first His kingdom and His righteousness, and all these things will be provided to you." (NASB 2020). In this verse, Jesus challenges us to seek His Kingdom and His righteousness. The Kingdom part comes easy. However, righteousness is complicated. Righteousness means to be right before God. Understand that the blood of Jesus paid the price for us to be righteous. We must position our circumstances from an attitude or stance of victory, not strive toward it, and completely surrender to God.

When anxiety controls us, we surrender to it. We fall into the trap of believing that anxiety is more powerful than God's righteousness. Having this mindset, we lose control, and the circumstances become more powerful than God's power. If you go about your day meditating on your anxious problem, you give up the ability to seek God's Kingdom and inhibit yourself from His righteousness. Focusing on anxious problems only makes them bigger. Understand that the identity we carry (Jesus Christ) is our righteousness.

Through Christ, we are righteous before God, and this creates courage. The courage to relinquish control and surrender to God allows us to live from our hearts and not our minds.

Seeking God's Kingdom starts with victory because you are righteous by the blood of Jesus. Ultimately, you will have the courage to live out your life from your heart. God cares about your heart posture; by walking in His righteousness, you will ultimately crush anxiety.

Looking Ahead to High School

The words from that conference room meeting and the constant pressure to fit into a mold had left their mark. As junior high wrapped up, I knew I was headed to high school, a new chapter with new challenges. But the thing about leaving one place for another is that you carry your past with you, whether you like it or not. I hoped high school would be a fresh start, a place where I could find my people and shake off the old labels, but a part of me knew it wouldn't be that simple.

High school had its own set of rules, its own social structure, and I was about to jump into the deep end. Sure, I was excited about learning to drive, the chance to make new friends, and maybe even the prospect of joining some cool clubs. But I also knew that I wasn't done with the struggle against rejection, the feeling of not quite fitting in, and the pressure to be someone I wasn't.

As much as I wanted high school to be a clean slate, I knew I would have to face some hard truths about who I was and where I belonged. The transition from junior high to high school wasn't just a physical move—it was an emotional and mental one too. I was still battling ADHD, still figuring out who I was, and still hoping to find inspiration from somewhere, anywhere.

Identity Crisis

The journey ahead was bound to be a mix of highs and lows, and I was ready for it—at least, I thought I was. It was time to take a deep breath and step into those high school halls, hoping I wouldn't trip over my own feet.

Key Takeaways

1. **Understanding and Addressing Rejection:** The conference room scene illustrates the impact of criticism and rejection on a student with ADHD. It's a reminder that educators should approach students with empathy and compassion, ensuring that feedback doesn't damage a student's self-worth. Constructive criticism should be paired with support and encouragement.

2. **Supporting Students Through Identity Struggles:** Chapter 5 explores the internal conflict students face when pressured to conform. Teachers and educators should encourage students to embrace their unique qualities. It's essential to recognize that each student's journey is unique and requires patience and understanding.

3. **The Importance of Inspiration in Learning:** This chapter underscores the role of inspiration in keeping students with ADHD engaged. Educators should consider creative teaching methods that go beyond traditional lectures and worksheets. Hands-on activities, interactive learning, and real-world connections can make a significant difference in culivating a student's interest.

4. **Managing the Stigma of ADHD:** The chapter discusses the negative perception often associated with ADHD and how it can impact a student's self-esteem. Teachers should be aware of the language they use and the messages they send, ensuring that students with ADHD feel valued for who they are, not judged by their diagnosis.

5. **Faith-Based Encouragement with the Help of the Holy Spirit:** Faith-based support plays a crucial role in encouraging students

through life's challenges. By embracing a perspective centered on Jesus Christ, educators and parents can offer students a sense of purpose and belonging. Seeking guidance through prayer and the Holy Spirit provides strength and courage to face adversity. Teaching students to rely on their faith fosters a deeper sense of community and compassion, reinforcing that they are not alone. Trusting in God's plan, while focusing on spiritual growth, can be a powerful way to help students navigate their unique journey with hope and confidence.

Reflective Questions

- How have your experiences in junior high shaped your relationship with God and your understanding of His plan for you?

- What insights have you gained about handling ADHD through faith?

Role-Playing Scenarios

Imagine revisiting a pivotal moment in junior high when your identity felt threatened due to ADHD.

- **Step 1:** Role-play how you might handle the situation now, integrating faith and a better understanding of ADHD.

- **Step 2:** Discuss or journal about how faith could have influenced your decisions and provided support during those challenging times.

Interactive Journal

- Reflect on a time when you felt God's presence during a challenging moment related to your ADHD in junior high. How did this experience strengthen your faith and self-identity?

- Write about a time when you felt misunderstood because of your ADHD and how turning to prayer or scripture provided comfort or clarity.

Prayer

Spend a moment in quiet reflection, then use the following prompts to guide your prayer:

- Pray for healing from any past hurts related to misunderstandings about your ADHD and ask the Holy Spirit to fill you with peace and understanding.

- Seek forgiveness for times you might have responded out of frustration or anger and ask for the grace to forgive those who may have hurt you.

- Thank God for the unique way He created you and ask for continued guidance in using your experiences and ADHD for His glory.

CHAPTER SIX

TRANSITION TO

HIGH SCHOOL

CHAPTER SIX

TRANSITION TO HIGH SCHOOL

Chapter Six

Transition into High School

Summer of 1995

Moving on to high school felt like a big deal—the kind of transition that makes you feel like you're entering a whole new world. This was supposed to be the start of something exciting, a chance to leave behind all the awkwardness of junior high and step into a place where I could redefine myself. But as much as I wanted high school to be this fresh start, it didn't take long to realize that it wasn't quite what had hoped for.

High school was just an extension of junior high, but with more pressure and more complicated social dynamics. I was still in LD classes, still couldn't make the basketball team, and still struggled to find my place. The biggest shock was that now I had to deal with three grades of older students, which made it tough to feel like I belonged. And on top of all that, my best friend, Josh, moved away, leaving me without my usual support system.

The lack of friends was the first major hurdle I had to overcome. Without Josh around, I had to find new people to hang out with. It wasn't easy. I spent a lot of time trying to impress others, hoping to find acceptance. The marching band became my refuge. It was where I found people who were just as passionate about music as I was. Being part of the band kept me busy, but it didn't completely erase the feeling of loneliness. I still wanted to be part of the "cool" crowd, but I just didn't fit in.

The summer of 1995, before my freshman year, the Charleston High School Marching Band was invited to play at the 4th of July parade in Washington, D.C. It was a big deal for a small-town band like ours. We spent the whole summer getting ready for that parade. What made it special was that the graduating class was also able to participate, which meant we had five grade levels of band members. We practiced every day, marching up and down the same road, eventually taking long routes around the city of Charleston, Illinois. I tried to make friends with the older grades, but it never seemed to work out. Even the crush I had on a girl who was a year older than me went nowhere. I felt like I was always on the outside, looking in.

The trip to Washington, D.C., was an interesting experience. My mom was a chaperone for a group other than mine, so she was nearby the whole time. It was difficult to talk to other band members because they were mostly juniors and seniors that I didn't know. Eventually, I joined the group my mom was chaperoning just so I would have someone familiar to talk to. Despite the awkwardness, the trip was memorable, and I realized I had to work hard if I wanted to fit in with my peers.

Walking into the Halls of High School

Freshman year presented a whole new level of challenges. I was mixed in with kids I didn't know, many of them juniors, which made things awkward. Physical Education and band were some of the classes where I shared space with these older kids, and it was tough to find my place among them. The lack of a traditional homeroom didn't help either; my homeroom was at the end of the day in a special education class, far from where most other freshmen gathered.

The teacher overseeing this class was a family friend, and I appreciated her support. But being in a small group with students known for causing trouble was uncomfortable. The classroom was located on the top floor, near a major stairway. Everyone could see who was in it. I felt like I was in the spotlight for all the wrong reasons. My friends from other classes would pass by and look at me with confusion, wondering why I was in this classroom. It felt like I was trapped in a space where I didn't belong.

Academic Limitations

One of the biggest disappointments during my freshman year was discovering how limited my academic options were. I desperately wanted to take chemistry, but the school told me I couldn't. I tried to push back. My mom intervened, but it was like hitting a brick wall. The school was adamant that chemistry was too hard for me, given my placement in special education. It broke my heart that I wasn't even given a chance to try, and I felt like I was being boxed in by the system.

It was frustrating to be told what I couldn't do, especially when I knew I had the capacity to learn. The rejection from not being permitted to take chemistry left a mark. It felt like the school was saying I wasn't capable of handling challenging subjects. It wasn't until much later in life, after I was married and had a career, that I learned chemistry on my own, proving to myself that I could do it. But at the time, being shut out of certain classes made me feel like a failure.

Choosing Between Band and Football

I didn't play football during my freshman year because I was so busy with band. Although I considered playing football, I understood that going to Washington DC with the band was a big deal. Missing football camp my freshman year would not go over well with the team, and playing football would mean missing out on marching band, which I loved. So, I made the difficult decision not to go back into football, even though I truly loved the sport and wanted to continue.

Instead, I decided to try out for another sport and gave golf a shot. Despite never having gone to a match, I made the golf team. I played and practiced with the team regularly and really enjoyed it.

Marching Band and Fifth Quarter

During the fall, I was heavily involved in the marching band. I enjoyed being part of the pep band at football games on Friday nights and working on mastering our halftime shows. Although it was challenging, we had a lot of fun.

One of the highlights of the year was Charleston's "Fifth Quarter," a place for kids to meet after home games. They had a DJ, music, and free pizza. It was hosted uptown. When Friday night rolled around, and we were to host a home football game, anticipation filled the air as everyone in the school looked forward to the afterparty at Fifth Quarter. When we won the football game, the afterparty was even better.

When the game ended, our marching band would march back to the high school to change out of our band uniforms and prep to head to Fifth Quarter. Everyone would be talking about it. One thing I always anticipated was the chance to talk to girls and even ask them to dance. Most of the time, I would boldly ask a girl from an older grade to dance with me. However, no matter how hard I tried, I was always rejected. I knew this was normal, but it seemed that the girls in my class only wanted to slow dance with the older boys. Being rejected for a slow dance was just a part of high school life, and I knew that. However, it was still very hard not to blame myself and my ADHD.

Basketball Tryouts

After football season ended, I decided to try out for the basketball team, thinking that maybe a different coach and a different school would give me a chance. I made it to the final cut. Even though I did really well, the coach sat me down and explained that he was cutting me because I didn't have as much experience as the other players did. He didn't foresee me doing well in the program. He told me in a way that wasn't hurtful. I respected him because he had been my brother's coach in high school, so I respected his decision as well.

I took it as another sign that maybe I wasn't good enough. My sporadic thinking and inability to stay on task due to ADHD worried me. I was tall, could jump, and could hit the rim of the basketball hoop, but I just couldn't compete with some of the other guys. I decided to try out for the team again the following year.

Concert Band and Jazz Band

In the spring of 1996, concert band picked up. I wanted to try out for jazz band, but my band director said I didn't have the skill set. It basically boiled down to the fact that I played alto saxophone, and there were too many alto saxophone players from the older grades with more experience. I didn't make the jazz band, so I turned my focus to concert band and absolutely loved it. Playing with other instruments while playing my own was surreal. You can go to a concert and hear the beauty of the music, but playing it gives you a whole new outlook. It felt like a romance with the music, —falling in love with the way you play, and interacting with each instrument, and watching the conductor.

Track and Field

When spring came around, I decided to join the track team. I had ran track in junior high, but I hadn't enjoyed it much back then. However, during my freshman year, I discovered a newfound passion for pole vaulting, a sport I dabbled in during eighth grade. That year, it really took off for me, and I found myself excelling in ways I hadn't before.

Pole vaulting was exhilarating. The 22 different movements executed in a span of two to three seconds, the rush of bending the pole, and the thrill of propelling myself high into the air was absolutely thrilling. I also participated in the high jump, which added another layer of excitement to my track and field experience.

Track became a place where I could channel my energy and focus, and it provided a sense of accomplishment and joy that was incredibly fulfilling. The blend of technical skill and sheer adrenaline made competing in track and field was one of the highlights of my freshman year.

Daily Life and Social Challenges

School days during freshman year came with their own set of challenges. The juniors and seniors had spacious lockers, while freshmen and sophomores were stuck with small, narrow lockers in the most crowded area of the school. Navigating through the packed hallways was often a struggle.

Finding a group of friends was also difficult. I ended up spending time with my bandmates, who were more like acquaintances than close friends. I often felt like I was trying to fit in and be someone I wasn't, just to gain their acceptance. I would do things I wasn't proud of to make them laugh, often becoming the target of their jokes just to get some attention. This routine became an almost daily occurrence during lunch, and it left me feeling isolated and misunderstood.

Despite these struggles, I did find solace in some areas of school life, particularly in the art room, which provided a much-needed refuge from the social pressures I faced elsewhere.

Finding Solace in Art

One of the things I enjoyed most in high school was the art program. Our art teacher was incredible, and I still interact with her a little bit on social media to this day. Being around creativity in any area was a lot of fun. There was everything from working on a potter's wheel to painting and drawing. I found myself more at home in the art room, which was in the basement of the school.

The art room became a safe place where I could truly express myself. With ADHD, I often struggled to stay on task in other areas, but art allowed me to enter into deep divergent thinking and hyperfocus. My divergent mindset let me explore my creativity in ways I couldn't elsewhere. Being creative and immersed in art always felt natural to me, and I thrived in that environment. So, I want to say thank you to my art teacher if she's reading this book.

Struggling with Acceptance

By the end of my freshman year, the constant rejection I felt from being in special education classes left me feeling like a loser. I truly enjoyed going to school and participating in activities like concert band, track & field, and art. These activities were so much fun, and I did not feel directly rejected when I participated in them. However, there was an underlying shame and guilt because I wasn't experiencing the academic side of high school like everyone else. I often worried about what others thought of me being in special education classes, and this feeling of not fitting in academically made me question my self-worth and why ADHD had to be such a problem for me. Despite my active participation in various activities, I felt like I was always on the outside looking in when it came to academics, which made me angry and resentful.

Living with these feelings of rejection and hurt built up a lot of frustration inside me. I remember waking up in the morning feeling anxious and uneasy as I got ready for school, partly because I was leaving the safe space of my home and heading into an environment where I felt vulnerable and out of place. Small things would easily upset me, and I often felt defensive throughout the school day.

During my freshman year, my dad was building a new church in our neighborhood. After the church was completed, we started attending services there. I grew up in a Baptist church but did not follow Jesus at all. Once we started going to this new church, I found myself attending the youth group. It was here I found friends that I actually enjoyed being around. Youth nights included worship music and a message from our pastor. It wasn't normal for me to enjoy something like this, but it felt so good to have friends and to have people pray for me that I continued to attend off and on through high school. Honestly, I wasn't really living for Jesus, but the youth group offered me a place where I felt welcome. It was a small community where I found friends and support, even if I wasn't fully committed to the faith yet. It helped me through some of the toughest times.

Finding Hope in Jesus Christ

I want to take a moment to address anyone going through a similar experience. If you're in high school and feeling like you're being held back, I want you to know that you're not broken. There's nothing wrong with you. The system might make you feel limited, but don't let that define who you are. If you have a dream, pursue it. Even if the system doesn't give you the tools, find a way to learn on your own. I learned chemistry later in life, and it was much more rewarding because I did it out of my own passion.

Through all these challenges, I've come to understand that having ADHD doesn't mean you're limited. It's just a different way of thinking that requires a bit more effort. If you're struggling with feelings of rejection or limitation, there's hope in Jesus Christ. He knows you and has a plan for your life. Don't let the academic system or anyone tell you what your limitations are. Trust in Jesus and let your heart guide you. You'll find that the rewards are far greater when you achieve something through your own determination and faith.

Summer of 1996 and Baseball

It was the summer of 1996, and I had just completed my freshman year of high school. One thing I haven't mentioned yet is that I played baseball, a sport that deeply connected me with my dad and brother. Growing up, we often played together, and as a family, we would go to St. Louis Cardinals games. I loved watching Ozzie Smith play and marveled at his athleticism, especially when he would do his signature backflips. Dad would always take us to the games, and sometimes Mom would join. However, during my college years, I ended up becoming a Cubs fan, much to the amusement and rivalry within my family—I'll just leave that one there.

I played in the city recreation baseball league since I was a little boy. Baseball was a great way to connect with my Dad during the summer and he would often be my head coach. I had two more years left to play city baseball and wanted to keep playing past that into my Junior year.

In the spring of my sophomore year, I tried out for the Charleston high school baseball team but didn't make it. I wanted to continue playing but hadn't played on the school teams in junior high or freshman year, which I probably should have. I did well in tryouts but the coach stated the cut was tough since I had three grade levels above me, each grade had players trying out.

I was sad about not making the team but it did not bother me as much since I still had two years of city league left to play. I simply just loved the game, it is one of those sports where things happen fast, but the game itself moves slowly. Whenever I was up at bat, I would overanalyze everything. I really think that was part of my divergent thinking and ADHD—I would overthink to the point of messing up.

This year in the city league was bittersweet. I vividly remember one game where I hit the ball to the fence. It was hard to hit home runs in the ball diamond we played in, but I came very close. I bounced the ball off the back fence in middle of center field, which was the deepest part of the field. Everyone noticed and wondered why it didn't go over. I wanted it to be a home run so badly. That moment made me realize that my time playing baseball was coming to an end, but I had achieved one of the hardest things to do in that league: I hit the ball to the fence.

Despite not making the high school team, these moments on the baseball field were significant. They represented my determination and passion for the sport. The skills and discipline I developed during those years stayed with me, shaping my approach to challenges in life. Baseball taught me about perseverance, even when the outcome wasn't what I had hoped for. It also taught me to find joy and accomplishment in personal milestones, no matter how small they might seem to others.

As I reflect on those days, I cherish the memories of playing catch with my dad and brother, the excitement of attending Cardinals games, and the laughter and rivalries that developed as I switched my allegiance to the Cubs. These experiences, both on and off the field, were foundational in shaping who I am today.

Returning to School and Gaining New Experiences

Summer came to a close, and I was entering my sophomore year. I picked up right where everything left off in my freshman year; not much had changed. In the fall, I continued with marching band but didn't play golf that year. I still had trouble with girls and being accepted among my peers.

One notable difference in my sophomore year was that I took an environmental science class, which I really enjoyed. The teacher was my former golf coach and knew my family well. His class was challenging, but I did well because it allowed creativity and a fun learning environment, similar to my science class experience in eighth grade.

I joined the Green Earth Society in high school and was selected to lobby in Springfield, IL, for the Coles County Soil and Water Conservation District. I had to read up on and explain issues related to soil and water conservation to our congressman. This experience felt great; it was an accomplishment that showed I could achieve something meaningful, something my peers in special education classes typically would not pursue due to lack of interest.

Using hyperfocus and divergent thinking, I navigated this task effectively, immersing myself in a state of optimal learning. I loved the outdoors and environmental science, and this experience was truly enriching. Later, in my junior year, I took an advanced environmental science class and succeeded.

Learning to Drive

In the spring semester of 1997, I began driver's ed. Finally, I was going to learn how to drive. I'll never forget the time Dad took me out to the country. He told me to get out of the car and get in the driver's seat, which I thought was weird since I was only 15 and didn't have my learner's permit yet. I was shocked and asked, "You want me to do what, Dad?"

Trying to drive for the first time, I hit the gas too hard, and Dad asked, "What are you doing?" Once I got the hang of it and started driving, I thought to myself, "My brain is working so fast right now with everything that is going on. How could I possibly make this work with ADHD?" I was laughing about it on the inside and loving the experience at the same time. It was a good experience and a memorable moment with my dad.

Key Takeaways

1. **Navigating Transitions:** Transitioning into high school exemplifies the challenges and growth opportunities that come with major life changes. Recognize the significance of adapting to new environments and how they shape personal development.

2. **Finding Community:** The importance of finding a supportive community, like a band or youth group, is crucial during periods of personal transition. These groups can provide a sense of belonging and help mitigate feelings of isolation or rejection.

3. **Role of Extracurricular Activities:** Engaging in extracurricular activities such as band, sports, or art provides valuable outlets for self-expression and skill development, and can significantly enhance the high school experience.

4. **Dealing with Rejection and Acceptance:** Learning to cope with rejection, whether in academic settings or social circles, is a pivotal skill. The experience teaches resilience and helps clarify one's values and identity.

5. **Spiritual Growth:** Encountering and overcoming personal and spiritual challenges can lead to profound spiritual growth and a deeper relationship with God. This can be particularly meaningful during formative years, offering guidance and comfort.

Personal Reflection

Reflect on your own experiences of transition, such as moving from junior high to high school or any other significant life change. Consider how these transitions affected your sense of belonging and identity.

- How did your expectations of a new phase in your life compare to the reality of it?

- In what ways did you feel supported or unsupported during these transitions?

Interactive Journal: Reflecting on Growth and Resilience

Reflect on the growth you experienced and note any resilience that occurred as a result of your experiences. Use the following prompts to guide your reflections:

Overcoming Challenges:

- What were some significant challenges you faced during a major transition in your life, such as moving to a new school, starting a new job, or moving to a new city?

- How did you manage these challenges, and what strategies did you find most effective?

Personal Growth:

- In what ways have you grown as a result of these challenges? Consider changes in your resilience, understanding of yourself, or your relationships with others.

- What have you learned about your own capacity for adaptation and overcoming adversity?

Prayer

Heavenly Father, I pray for Your guidance and strength as I navigate the transitions in my life. Help me to see these changes as opportunities for growth and learning. Grant me the wisdom to seek support when needed and the courage to step into new experiences with faith. Bless me with resilience to overcome challenges and the grace to find joy in every new beginning. Amen.

CHAPTER SEVEN

UPPER CLASSMAN YEARS

Chapter Seven

Upper Classman Years

Summer of 1997

It was now the summer of 1997, and I was going into my junior year. My youth group took a trip to see a Christian ska band at the Illinois State Fair. Ska is a Jamaican music genre that emerged in the late 1950s, blending American R&B and rock and roll influences with traditional Jamaican sounds like mento and calypso. Known for its upbeat tempo, syncopated rhythms, and horn sections, ska evolved through several waves. It was here I was inspired by a whole new world of music.

We were about to see the O.C. Supertones. They were on tour with their second album "Supertones Strike Back." As the band began to play, the whole crowd erupted and started to dance with an incredible amount of energy. We all can look back on moments that define us, and I was living one.

I remember standing there staring at the saxophone player and thinking to myself, "I play saxophone, why have I never heard anything like this before?" I would like to state that Christian ska music was way better than mainstream ska. At least in my opinion. I would go on to listen to and be inspired by many Christian ska bands throughout high school. Looking back, I know Jesus was involved here. He knew I loved music and that I had a lot of energy. It was as if He was pointing me in the right direction even though I was not really living for Him.

Junior Year Fall 1997

As summer came to an end, I looked back and realized that not only had I really enjoyed the Supertones concert at the State Fair, but I had also gained some Christian friends who, to this day, are still very influential in my life. However, the challenge I now faced was walking into the high school halls again in my junior year.

My journey into new friendships began with the marching band. Band camp was an early starter, even before the school year properly kicked off, bringing me face to face with the incoming freshmen. Despite knowing very few of the younger faces, I was keen on forging fresh connections. Amongst the new additions, a group of saxophone players caught my attention. Among them, Maggie resonated the most. She was exceptionally kind, immensely passionate about her saxophone, and she walked out her Christian faith. She sat next to me in band and over the months, she became a good friend. It was refreshing making friends and breaking the barrier of connecting with the opposite sex.

As the marching band formation practice kicked off, I vividly recall rehearsing on Trojan Hill field in Charleston, Illinois, perfecting our moves for the halftime performances at football games. I could feel the excitement in the air. It was electric! Our band was perfectly sized—not so small as to be overlooked, yet not so large that we lost our sense of camaraderie. This created an ideal environment where we stood out just enough, especially compared to bands from smaller schools. It also provided plenty of chances to build new friendships, including the incoming freshmen.

As the last notes of band camp faded away, I found myself contemplating what junior year in high school would hold for me. It was a milestone year, not just for me but for all juniors as it signified the larger lockers awarded to us in the main hall. No more long treks to the outskirts of the main building. It marked our ascension to upperclassman status. Over the summer, I passed a significant personal milestone as well. I got my driver's license. Unfortunately, not having my own car meant I couldn't drive to school like some of the other juniors and seniors. My mom would lend me hers occasionally, but that wasn't what preoccupied my thoughts. My major concern was about how my academic life might alter during this pivotal year.

Despite grappling with the decision, I chose to reduce my reliance on Ritalin, which swiftly backfired, particularly in my studies. My concentration rarely lingered on completing homework. Participation in class came easily to me if the topic was engaging, and I always pushed myself to stay involved during lessons. However, summoning motivation for schoolwork outside the classroom walls was a persistent struggle. Hence, my academic landscape remained mostly unchanged—I was still navigating through special ed classes and focusing on honing my math and reading skills. Truthfully, I needed to improve my math skills, but the reading? That was a different story. I simply wasn't applying myself in English or in crafting essays.

Our school, recognizing that special ed students like myself were not low-functioning but simply required different methods of learning, attempted an integrative approach. One particular teacher was designated to host a hybrid history class in the older building's basement, far from the rest of the history department located across the campus in a newer building. The idea was to mix "normal" students with special ed students who were assessed to fare well in this environment. Unfortunately, this setup didn't resonate with me as intended. It felt like everyone knew exactly why I was there, despite assurances of discretion. The classroom's location, a basement distant from the typical academic hustle, seemed a glaring beacon of our differences rather than a bridge to inclusivity. While this initiative was a well-intentioned academic gesture, socially, it only intensified feelings of isolation rather than alleviating them.

As autumn deepened, the tempo of marching band life accelerated. We found ourselves performing in various parades, energizing the air at festivals and homecomings across universities like U of I (University of Illinois) and EIU (Eastern Illinois University), right in our hometown of Charleston. Of course, the highlight was our own Charleston High School festivities. Whether it was marching down Trojan Way to Trojan Hill or playing at the football games, these moments brimmed with excitement. There was something incredibly thrilling about game days. Besides the fun of being with my marching band friends, the field was where I thrived. My neurodivergent mind reveled in the challenge of coordinating complex movements with music, focusing meticulously on details that perhaps others overlooked. While many of my peers played football or other sports, I found my joy in the half time performance of our marching band during those Friday night home football games. There was a unique thrill in navigating the field without markers, just estimating the space around us, moving briskly while ensuring my playing was pitch-perfect and keeping in time with the conductor's tempo. It was exhilarating!

After the excitement of the games, we would all march back to the school. Shedding our band uniforms, we'd head to the Fifth Quarter—a post-game gathering that felt like a slice of teenage paradise. Here, amidst the echoes of music, the chatter over pizza, sodas, and snacks, I found myself truly savoring the high school experience. It was in these moments, surrounded by my bandmates in a carefree environment, that I began to appreciate high school more than ever before.

The connections I made with my bandmates started to blossom into deeper friendships. I introduced some of them to a local Christian outreach—The Hangout. This place was designed as a sanctuary for young people, a Christian initiative aimed at connecting with non-believers, predominantly targeting teenagers. The Hangout was more than just a venue. It provided a wholesome alternative to the usual teenage pastimes, a safe space to just be and enjoy good company and music. I was particularly excited to bring Maggie to an event featuring the band Johnny Q. Public. But back then, I didn't fully grasp what it meant to be a Christian. I was mostly looking for acceptance, eager to enjoy the companionship and happy times with new friends. But deep down, I knew I hadn't completely given myself to God—there was a part of me I was still holding back.

My First Girlfriend

As the crisp air of late fall set in and our marching band season wound down, Maggie and I found ourselves seeking each other's company more frequently outside the confines of school. I often borrowed my mom's car to make the trip across town to her place. I vividly recall one late October evening when we decided to take a stroll—an escape from the chaos of her younger siblings and a chance for some solitude. It was during that particular walk that something shifted. We found ourselves reminiscing and laughing over marching band stories, and as the laughter faded, we somehow ended up holding hands. What followed was a long stretch of silence, filled only by the sound of crunching leaves underfoot, until I gathered the courage to break it. "Will you go out with me?" I asked tentatively. Maggie stopped, releasing my hand only to face me with a gentle smile. "I would like that very much," she replied.

Maggie was a girl whose life was deeply rooted in her faith and her family, values that immensely influenced me. She was the first person I genuinely cared for outside my family circle. Her selflessness was evident in the way she always prioritized others. Inspired by her, I found myself returning to church and getting involved in Christian community events. With Maggie, I felt cherished for who I was, rather than who I was trying to be—a lesson she imprinted on my heart.

Though our relationship eventually concluded after five months, we maintained our friendship and spoke often. Our breakup was one our friends also saw coming. The day we decided to end our romantic relationship and stay friends was a mutual decision. We realized that we had very different interests in what we wanted out of life. Our friendship would last through high school. We would still hang out in groups with our friends and still find ourselves laughing at silly things of our past.

Moving the clock up several years. I hadn't seen or spoken to Maggie since high school until we unexpectedly met at an all-campus Christian event at EIU in 2002. During my tumultuous senior year of high school, Maggie witnessed my downward spiral, and our communication had ceased since the spring of 1999. When I spotted her, I couldn't resist. I walked over and greeted her. Maggie was noticeably taken aback, surprised to see me there. Our initial conversation was stilted and awkward, but I quickly shared that I was now part of the Christian Campus House and had committed my life to Jesus. (The tale of my radical transformation will unfold in later chapters.)

Her reaction was a heartfelt hug, unlike a normal one. It reminded me of the ones we shared during our dating days, lingering and full of old warmth. As we finally stepped back, I noticed tears glistening in her eyes. "I never stopped praying for you," she disclosed, her voice thick with emotion. Overcome, she pulled me into another prolonged embrace, holding on tightly. After the event, we found a quiet spot outside and caught up for hours, reconnecting and rebuilding bridges long thought burnt.

Maggie and I exchanged stories, just like we used to, and I even shared my journey to finding Jesus with her. As we sat at the table, she held my hand tightly and, for some reason, I couldn't bring myself to let go. While rekindling our romance wasn't on my mind, I understood the significance of that moment and her answered prayers for me. As our conversation drew to a close, she came to sit next to me on my side of the round table outside. Clutching my arm, she rested her head on my shoulder firmly. Gathering my courage, I confessed, "Maggie, I love you but as a dear friend. At this stage in my life, I need to focus on growing with the Lord, not a romantic relationship." She sat up and looked at me intently, "I feel the same. But since I'll be leaving the state soon, can we just stay like this for tonight?" She asked. "As long as your siblings don't bother us, I'll stay with you until 10:00," I replied.

Maggie burst into laughter and embraced me tightly again. Curious, I asked, "Why all the big hugs and cuddles tonight?" She explained, "I ended things all those years ago because you hadn't committed your life to Jesus. That was a dealbreaker for me. I loved you, but I couldn't continue on that path. I never stopped praying for you to find your way. Now that you have, it's everything I ever wanted back then. I just want to savor this moment and express how proud I am of you. I'm not ready for a relationship with anyone, and I'm about to move away. But know that you'll always hold a special place in my heart as a dear friend."

Maggie and I enjoyed each other's company for the rest of the evening, catching up and finding closure. I apologized for my behavior during our senior year. Little did I know that night would be the last time I would ever see Maggie. Years later, the devastating news of Maggie's passing from cancer on October 31, 2007, reached me. Though she is no longer with us, her spirit lives on within me. Maggie planted a seed in my soul that has since grown into a strong rooted tree, a lasting legacy of the profound impact she had on my life.

Drinking and Quest for Social Acceptance

In April 1998, I landed my first job at a local fast-food joint, making a grand total of $5.15 an hour flipping burgers. It was exhilarating to finally earn my own money, to have the freedom to spend it as I pleased. Despite the thrill, the job came with its own set of challenges and introduced me to a complex world of workplace social dynamics. At the same time, I was navigating the demands of school and maintaining a social life, each element adding its own hurdles to my everyday existence.

An invitation to my first ever party arrived at a pivotal moment. It was a chilly weeknight in late April. The excitement was palpable as I walked into the house party where familiar faces greeted me — many from work. The refrigerator was loaded with beer. Our host handed one to me, popped it open, and cheerily dismissed any formalities. "Just take what you want."

Despite my limited experience with alcohol, that night I dove headfirst into the sea of inebriation. It was as if each sip was a steppingstone to a new, exhilarating identity. Beside me was a female coworker, someone I had quietly admired, a few years my senior. As the night wore on, our laughter mingled, and flirtation flared into a heated moment. Yet, even as the room spun and my inhibitions melted away, a core part of me resisted. I valued sexual purity—not out of religious obligation, but from a deeply personal conviction.

In a moment teetering on the edge of consequence, I pulled away, muttering goodbyes smeared with regret and inebriation. I stumbled to my car—a decision as reckless as it was dangerous—and somehow navigated the short drive home. I shouldn't have driven home in my inebriated state, especially not in my parents' car. But the party was close to our house, and I made it home. As I stumbled in, trying to quietly navigate the bi-level house, I found myself at the bottom of the stairs next to the front door, leaning against the wall for support. There, my mom met me with a worried look, asking if I was alright. Needless to say, I found myself in trouble and relieved from my driving privileges for a long while.

At the time, I was oblivious to the fact that this evening was the start of a disturbing trend. My quest for social approval steered me toward more frequent drinking sessions. Living in a college town, alcohol was never hard to come by, thanks to my older friends who were always around. Gradually, I found myself plunging deeper into a lifestyle fueled by alcohol, smoking (cigarettes had to be procured by others since I was under 18), and endless parties. It was a heady mix that was as intoxicating as the substances themselves, filling a void within me that craved attention, desire, laughter, fun, and acceptance.

Reflecting on these moments, I can see that what started as a pursuit of acceptance became a significant personal struggle, enveloping my lifestyle and choices during those impressionable years of my youth.

Summer of 1998

During the end of my junior year, I decided to get into skating. I loved rollerblading and playing roller hockey. It became an outlet for me, a place where I felt safe. It was just me and the roller blades moving. However, a few skating friends I had connected with introduced me to a whole new style of skating—Aggressive In-Line. It was super dangerous and super fun! I remember telling my dad I wanted to order skates with grind plates, small wheels, and a thick plastic body. He said, "What do you need that for?" I told him I wanted to get on ramps, half pipes, and slide down rails. The emotional response from my dad was one I would never forget. My dad was never a fan of me skating, not to mention he had busted out some of his teeth when ice skating as a kid. Being a parent now, I would cringe too. However, my dad helped me get the skates.

The skate community was not best known for staying out of trouble. We would skate on public and private property since we had no other options. We would wax down concrete ledges and handicap rails and make a mess of things. But in the summer of 1998, my dad worked on trying to make a difference in the skating community by helping to build a public skate park. I will never forget my dad generously using his carpentry talents to help us skaters create a home.

All the troubled kids that skated finally had a home and my dad was well respected for helping to build an amazing half pipe and skate park. Every time I visited the skate park, even a couple years into the future, kids would talk about my dad and how he stepped up to build us a nice skate park. My dad planted a wonderful seed in me that day. He showed me how to give back to the community and to offer help to those who were shunned by societal norms. Those skaters became my new community. I even started to work at another local taco restaurant that year. The taco restaurant was run by skaters and even managed by one. This was our home and hangout. It was because of my dad that I landed this job and was accepted into this group of friends. However, this group had a dark side too. Most of the older skaters were big drinkers and did some not-so-good things. Over time this took a toll on me, and I started to get noticed in high school as a "druggie."

The social push-back from my peers was horrible. I would retreat to the skate group, and we would fight back in destructive ways. We desperately wanted to be noticed but were going about it in all the wrong ways. When I think back on how I was feeling, I think about how misunderstood my group of skater friends were. We had our problems like every other clique or group of friends, but ours were just more publicly known. Being looked down on and always having something to prove made me feel even more rejected. The spirit of rejection had grown into a monster by the end of my junior year.

My First Car

The day I became the proud owner of a 1987 Dodge Shadow is the day my life changed gears. I had just wrapped up another shift at the local taco restaurant, a place that had become my second home where I was introduced to a group of friends who were more like family. As I tidied up, little did I know that my dad had orchestrated a surprise that would mark one of my most memorable days. I headed home in my mom's car from the day's work. When I arrived home my dad came and knocked on my door. "I will be back shortly. Please stay home and wait until I get back." My dad said yelling through my door. "I don't plan on going anywhere. I will be here when you get back," I replied yelling back through the door.

The minutes stretched and a curious blend of impatience and confusion bubbled within me. Then, from the perch of our second-floor window, a small white two-door coupe pulled into the driveway. My heart skipped. "That's Dad!" I nearly tripped over myself rushing downstairs, bursting through the door to confront the unexpected scene. "Dad, what is this?" I managed amid my shock. With a grin that stretched ear to ear, he handed me the keys. "This is your car. You'll pay for it by working at the taco restaurant." His words were a mix of pride and challenge. The surge of excitement left me practically airborne. I was ecstatic, overwhelmed with a tornado of emotions. At last the freedom I had long envied in my peers was mine to embrace. No more rides from Mom and Dad and no more borrowing Mom's car. "THIS IS AWESOME!" I said to myself in excitement.

This turbo-charged Dodge Shadow was more than just a car, it was my ticket to independence. As we took it out for its maiden voyage with me behind the wheel, Dad shared his thoughts. He saw my need for a car in my senior year, just as my brother had needed one. Dad spoke of responsibility too, reminding me never to drink and drive, to always abide by the law. Cruising down the street, the world felt different. I was no longer just a passenger in life. I was in the driver's seat, literally and metaphorically. And oh, how sweet the ride felt.

My Birthday and a Broken Nose

My birthday, nestled at the onset of summer in mid-June, was always a special time for me. Near the campus of Eastern Illinois University, there was a club frequented by college students—a lively dance venue adjoined to a restaurant, sprawling over two floors. Central to its charm was the vast pit where everyone danced while the DJ, stationed on the second floor, set the rhythm of the night. Alongside were nooks for lounging and socializing, making it the perfect enclave for youthful exuberance.

During those hazy summer months, the venue doubled as a haven for a high school outreach program. Teenagers from various nearby towns and communities converged there, swaying to music and sipping on non-alcoholic drinks. It was our safe space—a sanctuary away from the complexities of adolescence.

In that era of my life, my musical tastes had gravitated toward the heavier, grittier sounds. Nirvana topped my playlist and "Smells Like Teen Spirit" was my anthem. Whenever it played, my friends and I—goofy punk kids at heart—would launch into a frenzied mosh pit, reveling in the raw energy of the crowd. Most of the others steered clear, giving us a wide-open space. The next moment was one I would never forget. As my friends enjoyed our one song of the night, I collided with a familiar face—someone I admittedly couldn't stand. He shoved me hard, and I stumbled, tearing my favorite pair of jeans. I scrambled to my feet, fury coursing through me, and gave chase. But before I could confront him, a towering figure from another school interceded, shielding him. I tried to explain the situation, to make him see the injustice of the torn jeans—the betrayal—but he was unmoved. And when I attempted to sidestep him, he met my face with his forehead, and my nose cracked under the impact. Blood stained my favorite shirt, marking the moment forever.

That night, I called my parents from the club's landline—cell phones were a rarity then. Choking through tears and anger, I recounted how a shove led to my bloody nose. They were furious and pressed charges, which eventually led to a guilty plea from the guy who broke my nose. I never saw him again. Later that evening when I was home Mom and I spoke. "Are you okay?" my mom asked. "No, I'm not okay!" I yelled, looking the other way. I walked in a fit of rage to my room and slammed the door.

Reflecting on that night, I now realize the pain wasn't only physical. The feeling of helplessness, of being socially ostracized because I was the ADHD kid who thought differently, who was awkward—it all surged within me. That incident wasn't just about a broken nose or a ruined pair of jeans. It was a stark reminder of my place on the social ladder—the rejection that gnawed at me, urging me to find solace in escape, whether through friends, skateboarding, or just numbing the hurt away. I often found myself engaging more in booze and smoking cigarettes.

Rejection, Anger, Rage & Jealousy

As I look back, I am compelled to shed light on what was truly transpiring during that chapter of my life. My challenges with ADHD, academic struggles, and social connections had remained constant, but my heart and my attitude had taken a new shape. My junior year kicked off with a promising glint of excitement—I had a new girlfriend, and my outlook was bright. However, as I reached the middle of February in 1998, my life took a drastic downward spiral.

This period was a culmination of everything I had previously narrated about my childhood in this book. It was laden with the fury of being marginalized, the urge to retaliate brimming within, and a prevailing anger enveloping my daily existence. I am ashamed to admit that I mistreated several people close to me during this time.

Jealousy burrowed itself so deeply within me that I would often cry out to God in despair, questioning why I had to be different, why I had to struggle with ADHD. I sensed that in some way, God was reaching out to me through His divine, magnificent power, but my rage was a dense fog, obscuring my judgment, logic, and clarity of thought. Eventually, I succumbed to numbness. I didn't want to feel anything at all. This apathy extended to the people around me. I sought refuge in detachment, driven by an insatiable desire to simply drink, party, and immerse myself in frivolous fun. I genuinely lost concern for all else. What pained me most was how I succumbed to the notion of being an outcast, and I didn't just accept it—I embodied it. Looking on to my senior year I was marred with an attitude of defiance; an aura that screamed, "You don't like me, and I don't care. I'm going to show you just how bad I am because you've hurt me."

The nadir of it all was my surrender to the idea of rejection—not just grappling with it but allowing it to define me. Throughout my senior year, I paraded through the halls with a defiant attitude, a chip on my shoulder, broadcasting my indifference to whether or not people liked me. I was determined to showcase just how bad I could be, fueled by the pain they had caused me. This villainous identity wasn't naturally mine—it was a mask forged by the system, by societal judgments. It was a consequence of being denied a spot on the basketball team in 7th grade due to my academic challenges, and the constant branding of being different—a problem child—which relegated me to special education classes that never aligned with my intellect.

My life, during that turbulent period, had a singular focus—to mirror the pain inflicted upon me; to embody the very image of the 'problem child' they accused me of being, and to live out a reckless defiance in the face of a world that refused to understand or accept me.

Key Takeaways

1. **Impact of Christian Music and Community:** The chapter highlights the significant role that Christian ska music played in shaping my youth, providing a positive outlet and introducing me to a community that aligned with my energetic personality and spiritual needs.

2. **Challenges of ADHD in School:** It details my ongoing struggles with ADHD, focusing on the difficulties faced in academic settings and the importance of tailored educational approaches to support students with similar challenges.

3. **Beginnings of Substance Use:** This section marks the start of my experimentation with alcohol, illustrating how peer pressure and the desire for social acceptance led to increasingly risky behaviors.

4. **Role of Faith in Personal Struggles:** Despite drifting away, the presence of Jesus and the Holy Spirit is noted as a background influence in my life. Even as I faced challenges, the seeds of faith planted in earlier times remained potent, suggesting a path back to redemption.

5. **Influence of Positive Relationships:** The narrative explores how meaningful friendships, particularly with figures like Maggie who embody Christian values, can have a profound impact on personal growth and steer one toward recovery and self-discovery.

Personal Reflection

Reflect on the experiences shared in Chapter 7, which highlights key moments of personal growth and challenge during the upperclassman years. Consider these points to guide your introspection and journaling:

- **Influence of New Interests:** How have new interests or hobbies introduced during your formative years shaped your personal and social identity? Reflect on a time when you discovered a new passion and how it influenced your relationships and self-perception.

- **Consequences of Peer Influence:** Think back to a time when peer influence significantly impacted your decisions, for better or worse. How did those experiences shape your approach to friendships and social interactions later in life?

Interactive Journal

Reflecting on Growth and Choices

New Interests:

- Describe when a new hobby significantly impacted your life. What was it, and why was it impactful?
- How did this hobby influence your relationships and self-identity?

Peer Influence:

- Recall a time when peer pressure influenced a critical decision. What happened, and what was the result?
- How did this event affect your future social interactions and decision-making?

Prayer

Heavenly Father, thank you for Your ever-present guidance in my life, even when I stray from the path You've laid out for me. As I reflect on the times of change and the influences around me, I ask for Your wisdom to discern the right choices and the strength to pursue them, even when faced with peer pressure or challenging circumstances. Lord, please help me to find joy in wholesome interests and activities that enrich my life and bring me closer to You. Grant me the courage to resist the temptations that lead me away from Your will. I pray for Your protective hand over me, keeping me safe in challenging environments and guiding me back when I wander. Help me to see the lessons in every experience, good or bad, and to use these lessons to grow in faith, love, and understanding. May I always be aware of Your presence, seeking Your approval above all others, and let my life reflect Your love and grace. In Jesus name, Amen.

CHAPTER EIGHT

SENIOR YEAR

Chapter Eight

Senior Year

Out of Control Life

The summer of 1998 came to a close. Finally, my senior year was here! But by this time, I had spiraled out of control. I was smoking cigarettes and drinking alcohol, and later in the year started doing drugs. I will never forget going to my friend's birthday party in the country. That was the moment things went even darker for me. I found myself out in the woods with four other friends when one of them asked if I wanted to smoke some pot. I hesitated at first but then said yes. She handed me a pipe, and I smoked cannabis for the first time.

Because of this choice, I fell deeper and deeper into drugs and alcohol. Being the life of the party was my escape from reality. I gave up on trying to belong to something and turned to selfish desires. I did a lot of things I am not proud of and damaged a lot of relationships with people who truly cared about me.

As the school year progressed, I became more rebellious toward school, my family, and the church. I was living Satan's plan for my life at this point. I would find multiple ways to purchase alcohol and cannabis, and I continued to enjoy them. This was my identity, my lifestyle. I would listen to psychedelic music, everything from electronic trance to hard core metal with a bad message. I remember several times I would just walk out of school, get in the car with friends, and go out to an abandoned highway bridge and get drunk or high. When engaged in school activities, I would be defensive with my teachers and peers. When someone would look at me the wrong way, I would want to lash out and defend myself. I would often get into fights. It was an all-out war for my identity. When leaving school, I would light up a cigarette and make sure others would see me do it.

I had completely stopped taking my ADHD medication and would often give it to my friends. I would think of myself as better than others for having ADHD. Being able to think quickly and react fast came so easily for me with ADHD. However, the darkness in my life had blanketed any hope I might have had to try to make myself and my ADHD better. The darkness in my life finally manifested into rage. Uncontrollable rage. I would lose myself in it. The rage was intoxicating and made me feel powerful. I always wanted more. Rage became the only thing that would bring the attention I wanted from others. During this time in my life, I hurt a lot of people. My parents had no idea what to do with me. I was beyond the capability to find help in any way. Eventually the rage matured into a constant suffering for attention.

In all reality, I was hurting in a way that was the result of trying to be someone God did not create me to be. The problems in my heart and mind became bigger than what I thought God could do in my life. The biggest hurt was relationships in general. Every time I would engage in a relationship that was new, I would default to the position of anger and having to justify my ADHD behavior, or I came with the idea of having something to prove.

Imagine being in a constant state of having to prove yourself to everyone in your life. Furthermore, take that idea and mix it up with ADHD and trying to prove you're normal. Honestly this is probably the biggest and hardest struggle for those who have ADHD. Looking back now I can see I was partnering with:
- ✓ Rage
- ✓ Jealousy
- ✓ Insecurity
- ✓ Loneliness in relationships
- ✓ Destructive behavior

The only cure for this checklist as it pertains to ADHD is Jesus Christ. You see, Jesus is the identity of your relationship with God. If you have no relationship with Jesus, you have no relationship with the Father. Jesus said: "If you know me you know the Father." "Whoever has seen me has seen the Father." *John 14:7 & 9*

Not really knowing Jesus, my ADHD spiraled out of control my senior year. But having Jesus in my life now, living in my true identity, and having stepped into being so comfortable in my own skin by knowing who I am in Jesus Christ, I can now see the insecurities of others. Back then, when I would often make the insecurities of others my own, I wanted to solve those insecurities so I would be seen as normal based on everyone else's world view of me.

Here is the checklist I now have in my life. Let's compare it to my previous one:

- ✓ Joy and Peace
- ✓ A Generous Spirit
- ✓ Firm foundation in Christ and I know who I am.
- ✓ Loving and fruitful relationships
- ✓ Loving Behavior

Laying this out, you can now see that Jesus is the answer for ADHD. I still live with ADHD. It is still a part of me. I would not know what to do if it wasn't. I love who I am and love having ADHD. I love stepping into uncharted territory with Jesus by being a better steward of my mind.

"Do not be deceived. 'Bad company ruins good morals.'"

1 Corinthians 15:33

High School Graduation and Community College

In May of 1999, I graduated high school, only to find out that the life I had built dissolved. Most of the people I associated with began to move away. They disappeared from my life. I was left asking myself, "Where do I go from here?" I decided to enroll at Lake Land College in Mattoon, Illinois.

The summer of 1999 was coming to an end. I made many friends that summer. Most were people I drank or did drugs with. I had made friends with people older than me who could buy me alcohol. I even used them for a place to party and to stay when I was too intoxicated to go anywhere else. My path was still destructive, but a beacon of hope came to light later that fall.

Toward the end of high school, I started to enjoy rollerblading. Why am I bringing this up again? To answer, I would say I skated toward my salvation. In the summer of 1998, I started to get into aggressive in-line skating—the type of thing that would make any parent cringe in 1998. Sliding down handicap rails, going down half pipes, and even being daring in heavy traffic. This led me to a skating rink in Mattoon, Illinois. This is where I met a man named Jeff.

I started going back to Monday skate nights. You see, Monday nights were Christian skate nights at the rink. I started going to them when Maggie and I were dating. But now, something in my heart was drawing me back. Even though I was doing drugs and living a reckless life, I still had the seed in me that Maggie planted back in 1997. Because of Maggie's influence, I wanted to go back and experience what I had lost long ago.

After meeting Jeff, we discovered that we had so much in common. We both loved video games, and we both loved to skate. But Jeff also loved Jesus. I often remember when we were out skating in public, I would say some pretty harsh profanities. Jeff would simply say, "Dude! Watch your mouth!" However, Jeff never judged me or treated me any differently. He simply steered me in the direction of Jesus and empowered me to make good choices.

Come Follow Me – My Salvation

At that juncture in my life, I had abandoned my academic pursuits. One of my teachers had explicitly asked me not to return, largely because I was either a disruption or I attended class under the influence of drugs. At the same time, I was involved with a new girlfriend. However, everything changed on November 2, 1999.

I was on my way to drop my girlfriend off at her dorm at Eastern Illinois University. The drive back was unusually difficult. During the trip, she revealed to me what she learned from our friends we had just left—that I was growing cannabis and using drugs. She was furious. When we arrived at her dorm, she turned to me and said, "I am breaking up with you, and we are done." Her words shattered me. She didn't even allow me to defend myself. I was in utter shock! As the car door slammed shut, she walked away without looking back. It was clear to me then that it was truly over. Still in shock I just sat there. I got very angry. I started to blame my friends for revealing the information about my drug life to my girlfriend. The feeling of rejection set in, and I started to collapse with emotions as tears started flowing from my eyes.

I drove across the street and parked in the college parking lot next to the intramural fields. Still reeling from the shock, I began to reflect on my life, tracing back to my junior high days. I spoke aloud to myself, questioning, "WHY?" It seemed I would never be part of anything meaningful. I knew in my heart that my life was a mess, and I was a complete wreck. I stepped out of the car, put on my trench coat, and started walking toward a dark, vast field nearby. As I wandered deeper into the shadows, rain began to fall. I pondered despairingly, "Is this it? IS THIS WHAT MY LIFE HAS BECOME!?"

Suddenly, a powerful, earth-shattering voice pierced through my thoughts, calling out my name—just my name. Overwhelmed, I fell to my knees in the muddy ground, recognizing this as the voice of God. Speechless, I listened. Vivid images of what my life could be flashed before me—I saw myself making a real difference in the world. "What do I do?" I finally managed to utter.

"Come follow me," God instructed. "Give up all your friends, the drugs, the lifestyle, and follow me." At that very moment, I surrendered my life to God. Tears streamed down my face as an overwhelming sense of peace enveloped me. The love and the vision God shared filled me with a newfound purpose. He had laid out the path before me. All I had to do was walk it. "What do I do now?" I asked.

"Go home and tell your mom everything. Tell her you need help cleaning out all the junk in the house. She will be waiting for you when you arrive," God responded.

I stood up, wiping the tears and rain from my face, and started walking back to my car. I made my way back to my car, opened the car door and sat down in the driver's seat. I didn't drive away. I just sat there and started to reflect on all that just happened. Looking back on the whole experience, the most profound moment came when God reached out to me in my deepest despair. I'm not sure if it was my time to surrender my life to Him or simply a cry for help, but everything changed after my girlfriend broke up with me. The pain was unlike anything I had ever felt, and as I collapsed to my knees, overwhelmed, the Holy Spirit filled my consciousness. Still sitting in my car, I started to reflect on what the Holy Spirit just showed me in that field.

What the Holy Spirit showed me that night was vivid, borderless images flashing before my eyes—some of these visions have since become reality, while others, as of 2024, remain unclear and difficult to understand. It was then that I truly connected with God for the first time, and He promised, "I'm going to take what the enemy meant to destroy you—your ADHD, your life, all of it—and use it for good."

Driving home later, my mind raced with questions. Had I really heard the voice of God? As I parked and walked to my front door, anxiety gripped me, but what awaited inside was a moment of tender grace. Opening the door, I found my mom at the bottom of the stairs. Without a word, I stepped forward and we shared a long hug. Tears streamed down my face as I poured out my experiences to her. She revealed her own fears, telling me, "I was having trouble sleeping, fearing something terrible had happened to you. But then, I heard God reassure me that you were safe and that He had great plans for you." This confirmation from my mom underscored the divine intervention I had experienced. That night, I slept more soundly than I had in months, comforted by the transformative power of God's grace in my life.

A New Name for a New Creation

When I embraced this transformation, I changed my name from Jason to Jake because I was such a new creation that Jason felt foreign to me. The change was not immediate but something that I decided to do in the later weeks. It's no disrespect to my family; I'll still respond to that name. But after giving up everything to follow God, even my name had to change. Many of you knew me as Jason, but I became Jake because every time someone called me Jason, it just didn't feel right. I don't hate that name, but I gave it up to follow God.

Building a Relationship with God

Giving your life to God might feel exhilarating for a few months, but if you haven't cultivated a relationship with Him, it will falter, like trying to date someone without spending time together. People often ask, "How can I grow deeper and closer to God? How do I handle this problem or that issue?" My response is simple: ask God first. Most people would rather think about it before praying, but I always encourage them to pray first, then think—or just pray and act.

Key Takeaways

1. **Escalation into Darkness:** Acknowledge the devastating effects of succumbing to peer pressure, which lead to substance abuse. Understand the importance of making choices that align with God's plans, rather than those that lead to self-destruction.

2. **Impact of Lifestyle on Identity:** Reflect on how a lifestyle centered around drugs and alcohol can distort one's self-image and relationships, emphasizing the need for a true identity found in Christ.

3. **Power of Jesus in Breaking Chains:** Recognize the transformative power of Jesus Christ in breaking free from the chains of addiction, anger, and a destructive lifestyle. Embrace the Holy Spirit's role in renewing one's mind and spirit for a resurrected life in Jesus.

4. **Renewal through Divine Intervention:** Appreciate the pivotal moments of divine intervention that redirect life's path toward salvation and true purpose. Cherish the clarity and peace that come from surrendering fully to God's call.

5. **New Identity in Christ:** Embrace the profound change that comes from a relationship with Jesus, understanding that it can lead to such a significant transformation that one might feel led to a new name, symbolizing a new creation in Christ.

Personal Reflection

- Reflect on a time when your life felt out of control. What were the circumstances that led there, and how did they affect your relationship with God and others?

- Consider how identity and lifestyle choices impacted your relationship with God. How did embracing or resisting change shape your path?

Interactive Journal

- Transformation Documented: Write about a period in your life when you felt most distant from God. What led to that distance, and what were the consequences?

- Rediscovery of Faith: Reflect on a moment when you felt God's intervention. How did this experience change your perspective and actions?

Prayer

Heavenly Father, I come before You in humility, acknowledging my past mistakes and the times I walked away from Your light. Lord Jesus, thank You for Your grace that rescues us from the depths of despair and sets us on a path of righteousness. Fill me with the Holy Spirit and guide me away from the temptations that lead to destruction. Help me to embrace the identity You have for me in Christ, breaking free from the chains of my past. Let Your love and light be a beacon for my journey, transforming my heart and renewing my spirit. Amen.

CHAPTER NINE

NEW LIFE AS A CHRISTIAN

Chapter Nine

New Life as a Christian

The Shift

Things in my life had shifted. This wasn't just a small change, but a huge one. I had cut ties with all my friends, stopped the drugs, stopped drinking and smoking, and cleaned up my life. Anyone who has done what I just mentioned knows that this is difficult. Going "cold turkey" from all the smoking and drugs alone was hard. However, having Jesus in my life made things much easier. I remember sitting in my basement living room and getting a call from someone that I used to call a friend. I answered the phone, and he said, "Hey! Do you have any weed?" I replied, "I don't do that stuff anymore, and I am a Christian now." My old friend pretty much disconnected the call. At that moment, I quickly realized how much my life had changed. The concept of "you are a new creation" became a reality.

I realized at that moment I didn't have any friends. I never stopped to think if the people I was hanging out with were truly my friends. I can confirm— they did not care for me at all. This was rather challenging for me. Being social was a huge part of who I was. Choosing not to hang out with the old crowd of friends was a choice I made when I gave my life to Christ. I never knew how much my identity was rooted in my social life. However, something was different now; it was a powerful comfort in my mind that everything was going to be okay.

In that moment, I realized that my choice to give my life to Christ was a bigger change than I initially thought. I knew if I was challenged with cutting ties with all my friends and I did not have Christ in my life, things would be different. I would be feeling a sense of urgency to reconnect with my friends. Even though I had comfort from God, I still had a hole in my life that needed to be filled. I needed to find new friends—the right friends who would build me up in my new walk with Christ.

Cutting ties with my old friends was not my only challenge. The day after I gave my life to Christ, I stood in my bedroom. My bedroom was my safe place. However, my safe place did not seem so safe anymore. As I looked at my stash of cigarettes, alcohol, drugs, and pornographic magazines and videos, I started to have a sense of disgust. Normally, I would not think anything about my stash. But the change in my mind was so radical that I was disgusted with the sight of it all! I knew I had to rid myself of these things, but the humiliation of showing my own mother everything was making me tremble in fear. It was in that moment I remembered God would use my own mother to help me clean up my life. So, I realized this is what God meant when He said, "Go home and tell your mom everything." I worked up enough courage to talk to my mom and ask for help.

November 3, 1999, was a Wednesday, and I don't remember if my mother took the day off or not. I only remember her being around that day. She gave me encouragement and a trash bag. As I began to throw away my stash, I felt something die inside. The feeling of attachment that I once had to my former lifestyle was no longer there. I felt the presence of God around me as I continued to clean out the remains of my old life.

Each item that went into the trash bag felt like a weight lifting off my shoulders. Cigarettes, alcohol, drugs, and pornographic magazines and videos—all of it represented chains that had held me captive for so long. As they disappeared into the bag, I felt a profound sense of freedom. It was as if

God Himself was guiding my hands, helping me to rid my life of these burdens.

My mother stood by me, silently praying and offering support. Her presence was a reminder of the unconditional love that surrounded me, both from her and from God. Together, we filled several trash bags with the remnants of my past. By the time we finished, my room looked different, not just physically, but spiritually. It felt like a place where I could truly begin anew.

This cleansing process was more than just getting rid of physical objects; it was a symbolic act of surrendering my old life and embracing my new identity in Christ. The Holy Spirit was at work in me, transforming my heart and mind. I knew that this was just the beginning of my journey, but it was a crucial first step. With my room now free from the things that had once held me back, I felt ready to move forward and fully embrace the new life that God had in store for me.

Visit to Rehab

It was a sunny Thursday on November 4, 1999, when my mother suggested that I meet with a professional at a rehabilitation center in Champaign. I remember driving up with her and feeling a sense of confusion—why did I need to see a professional? As we pulled up to the campus, I decided to do this alone, without my mom. I wanted the professional to hear my side of the story.

As I entered the waiting room, I felt the presence of God fall over me. In that moment, I felt the Lord rewire my brain, and I started thinking about my future rather than my past. I entered the consult room, sat on a couch, and began speaking with the doctor. He started asking me general questions about alcohol and drug abuse. I replied that I had thrown all the stuff away and that it had been my choice.

The doctor seemed unconvinced and started asking about the change. I then told him about the previous Tuesday night when I gave my life to Jesus Christ. I explained that I gave up all my friends, social activities, and stopped all the drugs, alcohol, and cigarettes. I remember the look of disbelief on his face. The doctor finally asked if I would be willing to be admitted to the facility. At that moment, I had such a strong conviction that going there was not the right path for me.

The doctor was happy that I had turned a new leaf but urged me to be admitted, stating that they had a strong program to help make the changes I needed in my life. Just as I was about to sign the paper, I felt a still, small voice in my mind saying, "This is about money and not about you." The voice was the same as the one I heard the night I gave myself to Christ in the field. I dropped the pen on the clipboard and handed the form back to the doctor.

He asked, "Why did you not sign this?" I explained, "I just told you my entire reason for my change, and you did not believe me. I am better now in Christ Jesus." He countered, stating that he had seen people say the same thing to get out of it. I replied, "Did those people choose to give up everything? Because I did—my friends, my way of life, everything." At that moment, I told the doctor we were done. He stated he would like to talk with my mother since she dropped me off. I said, "I am an adult, and I have the right to deny your services. I would like to leave now." The doctor had no choice but to let me go.

I walked to my mom's car, opened the door, and sat down. She asked, "How did it go?" I said, "They kept trying to get me to sign to be admitted. I chose not to sign because I did not need the treatment or rehabilitation. I gave my life to Christ, and that is the life I am going to live now." Mom said, "Okay," and we started to drive home.

Positive Changes

One weekend, I was working at a taco restaurant in Mattoon, Illinois, at the drive-thru when, lo and behold, my childhood friend whom I hadn't seen since I was eight years old pulled up. "Are you Steve Letner?" I asked. "Yes, who are you?" This was another defining moment that started my new journey as a Christian. It felt like an answered prayer. I always loved hanging out with Steve when we were kids in first grade. He moved away, and I never thought in my wildest dreams that he would show up at my work in the drive-thru just a week after I gave my life to Christ.

Steve and I exchanged contact information, and he invited me to his church for Wednesday night Youth Group. I immediately said I would love to come. We spoke on the phone the next day, and I explained to him that I had given my life to Christ and given up all my friends. It was a conversation I will never forget. I told him that he was an answered prayer and that because he walked a Christian lifestyle and we were friends in our childhood, this meant so much more to me.

I met up with Steve on Wednesday night and went with him to his youth group. At first, I felt a bit old since I had just graduated high school. But that didn't stop me, and I embraced this new venue with an old friend. As I walked into the church building and headed downstairs, I couldn't help but ask why Steve had his guitar with him. "Why do you have your guitar?" I asked. "I lead praise and worship for youth group," he replied. "That's pretty awesome! I play saxophone," I said. He was super excited and said, "We should jam out sometime." "Sure, let's do it!" I responded.

The service started, and Steve introduced me to the group of about 30-40 people. I was asked to say a few words about who I was and my reason for coming to the group. I took the microphone and shared how God met me in a field and how I gave my life to Him. I also explained my past and how I gave it all up to follow Jesus.

Many of the group members were inspired by my story and introduced themselves after the service. They reached out to me during the week, inviting me to hang out. Steve also started coming over and spending time with me at my house. For the first time in my life, I finally found a place where I belonged. I didn't have to prove myself to anyone in my new circle of friends. I was simply loved.

I embraced my new friends and social activities. It was like a breath of fresh air. The people around me loved me, and my family was starting to notice the change in the people I was hanging out with. One weekend afternoon, I passed my parents' bedroom and saw my dad lying on the bed reading his Bible. I went upstairs and said to my mom, "Dad is reading his Bible! I've never seen him study God's word outside of church." Mom said he had seen such a positive change in me that he was reading his Bible more. In that moment, I realized that my transformation and walk with God positively influenced the people around me. This was very encouraging to me.

Time went on, and I started a ska band with Steve. We wrote music together and played a lot of shows. We even recorded two albums together. God was so good to even restore my childhood friend Jesse in my life, and he joined the band in 2001! The story is a good one. However, my struggles in the early days of the band were hard on me. The truth is, being a new Christian and having the attention from others was starting to wear off. Before Jesse joined the band in 2001, I had real struggles and almost lost it all.

The Spillway

In 2000, Steve and I formed a band with his friends, who also became my friends. Around the same time, I started settling into life at the First Assembly of God in Mattoon, Illinois. I was fitting in well, participating in their youth group despite being a college-age freshman. I found a sense of belonging I had never experienced before.

Steve invited me to play saxophone for the youth group's worship band, and I joined the praise band for the main services as well. But as time passed, I found myself deeply struggling. Despite having new friends and feeling God's restorative touch in my life, I was in considerable pain. All the rejection and emotional baggage from my past life weighed heavily on me as I transitioned into my new Christian life. This was exceedingly difficult.

I distinctly remember a day in the summer of 2000 when I hit rock bottom. The withdrawal symptoms from alcohol and cigarettes were overwhelming. Stepping away from the party lifestyle and its quick fixes was proving to be a tough challenge. At my lowest, I felt the enemy's strong presence in my life, trying to destroy me through a pervasive spirit of rejection that I had yet to confront. This led me to Charleston, Illinois, where the Embarras River meets Lake Charleston. At the spillway—a notorious spot where four others had lost their lives—I contemplated ending my own life.

Overwhelmed with pain, I desperately sought a sign of love and hope. "God, show me something," I pleaded. I had a basic, prepaid cellphone with me (this was before the era of smartphones and texting). I reached out to Steve, although I was supposed to be on my way to band practice. Confused and angry, my conversation with Steve was incoherent. Later, unable to explain my actions, I impulsively called my parents to say I was ending my life—a decision has that left a scar on my heart.

I turned off my phone, slipping it into my pocket as I approached the powerful, deadly waters of the spillway. Just before I could reach the edge, my powered-off phone rang. It was my youth pastor, Brett, who urgently asked, "What are you doing?" Startled, I remembered my earlier plea to God saying, "show me a sign." It was both God and Brett who intervened to save my life that day.

Following this incident, I avoided delving into the details with others but took time to reflect on my life with God's guidance. He revealed insights about my ADHD and its impact on my life, helping me realize the need to transform my struggles into strengths.

The Band That Is – The Saints

Summer 2001 marked a turning point in my life as my friendship with Steve and the band blossomed into a remarkable ska band ministry. Our common goal of spreading the message of Jesus Christ through our music brought us closer than ever before. We poured our hearts into recording songs, performing shows, and using our talents for the glory of God. This newfound sense of purpose and community ignited a transformation within me.

Weekends became a tradition of band practices as we gathered in Jesse's garage, writing music, and praying together. It was during these sessions that our bond grew stronger. We supported and encouraged one another, pushing ourselves to new heights both musically and spiritually through the Holy Spirit. Being part of a band that played for Jesus was an unforgettable experience that I will always cherish.

Over four years, we embarked on incredible journeys, traveling to neighboring states, recording two albums, and even playing a side stage at the Cornerstone Music Festival. I took up the saxophone and worked alongside Jesse, who was not only a talented musician but also an exceptional artist. His ability to create mind-blowing horn parts inspired me to push myself to new limits. I often questioned if I could ever reach his level of skill, but I learned to trust in Jesus and rely on His strength to surpass my own limitations.

Jesse's presence in the band not only pushed me musically but also held me accountable. His expectation of musical excellence motivated me to give my all. Together, we formed an unbreakable bond that propelled us forward in our musical journey, all while knowing that our ultimate purpose was to honor and serve Jesus. Those years spent in the band were some of the most meaningful in my life, leaving a mark on my life that will always be cherished.

ADHD, Creative Hyperfocus, and Playing in a Band

As an artist with ADHD, I have always felt a natural connection to music. The ability to flow seamlessly from writing to performing to entertaining is something that comes effortlessly to me. Playing in a band, particularly a Christian ska band, has allowed me to tap into a deep sense of fulfillment and mental stimulation.

The adrenaline rush I feel when performing in front of an audience is exhilarating. The urge to entertain and captivate the crowd merges with the creative flow between my bandmates. Every note, every drumbeat, and every dance move become an expression of our shared passion. It all happens so quickly and effortlessly.

Playing music has been both a joy and a challenge for me. As someone with ADHD, seeking attention from others is second nature to me. However, the spotlight being on me, whether in front of five people or hundreds, is both intoxicating and intimidating. This struggle, coupled with other obstacles, has often made it difficult for me to work harmoniously with my fellow bandmates, especially while on the road.

During my years in the band, I faced significant personal challenges. I hurt one of our band members, and it took years for us to forgive each other. Even today, our relationship has not fully recovered. Being unmedicated throughout my time in the band presented its own set of difficulties. While I am uncertain why I stopped taking my Ritalin, I found that my ability to focus was enhanced in moments of hyperfocus. In these instances, I became the driving force behind the band, organizing practices and propelling our creative process forward.

My ADHD has been both a gift and a burden. Organizational skills were not my strong suit, except when it came to something I loved, like being in my band. Music became the platform for me to showcase my abilities. During these moments, I felt a deep sense of pride and a spiritual connection to the

Holy Spirit. Whether practicing, writing music, or performing, the connection we made with others was truly extraordinary.

However, the band faced its own challenges. Losing our bass player, Phil, in the third year was a blow to the group. While we managed to find a replacement in Owen, the dynamics were never quite the same. Phil had a commanding presence, always pushing us to better ourselves, and his absence created a void. Despite having incredibly talented musicians in Steve, Jesse, and Bob, we were uncertain of what the future held for us.

When I took over as the band leader, admittedly I struggled to navigate the responsibilities that came with it. My ADHD made it challenging for me to control my emotions and stay focused on the band's objectives. However, I recognized that the combination of ADHD, creativity, and hyperfocus made me an unstoppable force when writing music. When the Holy Spirit was involved, there was a unique and profound connection. It is no wonder that worship-leading and creative music writing in churches flourish. Those with ADHD, like me, truly thrive in these environments. It feels like we are dancing with the Lord, both in our minds and in our bodies.

My journey as an artist with ADHD and a member of a band has been one of constant discovery and growth. While there have been challenges and moments of turmoil, the power of music and the connection it fosters are unparalleled. Through it all, I have learned to embrace the unique aspects of my ADHD and harness my creative hyperfocus to create something truly extraordinary on stage.

My Testimony and a Microphone

During my time in the ska band, we traveled to a venue called Joshua's Cup in Crawfordsville, Indiana. We played there many times and loved performing with the kids. Many popular artists played at this venue. During a second visit on December 8, 2001, I had the chance to share my testimony after we played the show.

This was the first time I ever spoke to a crowd about Jesus based on my life. After it was over and everyone was just hanging out having fun, a girl and her friend came up to me while I was with one of my bandmates. She started to explain that she was going through some tough times and was struggling with some decisions she had made. She kept asking the right questions about Jesus and living a new life in Him. After about half an hour she accepted Jesus into her life for the first time. This was also the first time I led someone to Jesus. The Joshua's Cup venue was a local outreach and only booked Christian bands for this purpose. Having someone come to Jesus by telling my testimony really shook me in my head space. As the news reached the rest of the band, we all celebrated with her.

The ride home from Crawfordsville was long. Sitting there in the van I was quiet. This was very unusual for me. I kept to myself and kept thinking about how God moved through my story to reach and save a troubled girl. This was one of the biggest highlights of my life in the band and I still remember it vividly to this day.

Key Takeaways

1. **Radical Transformation Through Christ:** Embracing a new life in Christ brought about a radical transformation, leading to the rejection of old habits and friendships that did not align with this new path.

2. **Supportive Community:** Finding a supportive Christian community was instrumental in fostering spiritual growth and providing a sense of belonging that was previously missing.

3. **Struggles and Rejections:** The transition to a Christian life involved significant struggles, including dealing with past rejections and emotional baggage, but it also highlighted the importance of perseverance and faith.

4. **Impact on Others:** The changes in my personal life positively influenced family and friends, showcasing the transformative power of living a Christ-centered life.

5. **Creative Hyperfocus in Ministry:** Utilizing ADHD-driven creative hyperfocus can lead to profound spiritual and communal connections, serving as a testament to God's work through personal challenges.

Personal Reflection

Take a moment to reflect on your own life. Have you ever experienced a significant transformation? How did it affect your relationships and daily habits? Reflect on the following questions:

- **Transformation:** Have you ever undergone a major life change? What was the catalyst for this transformation?
- **Support System:** Who are the key people in your support system that help you grow spiritually and emotionally? How do they impact your daily life?
- **Challenges:** What are some challenges you faced during your transformation? How did you overcome them?
- **Influence:** Think about how your transformation has influenced those around you. Have you noticed any positive changes in your family or friends?

Interactive Journal

- **Document Your Change:** Write about a significant transformation in your life. What was the turning point?
- **Identify Your Support System:** List the people who have supported you through your journey. How have they helped you grow?
- **Overcoming Challenges:** Detail the challenges you faced during your transformation and the strategies you used to overcome them.
- **Impact on Others:** Reflect on how your transformation has positively influenced your family, friends, and community. Write about specific instances where you noticed these changes.

Prayer

Heavenly Father, thank You for the power of transformation through Jesus Christ. I pray for the strength and courage to let go of old habits and friendships that do not align with my walk with You. Help me find a supportive community that fosters spiritual growth and provides a sense of belonging. Guide me through the struggles and rejections, and help me see the positive influence my transformation can have on those around me. Thank You for using my unique challenges, like ADHD, to glorify Your name and serve Your purpose. In Jesus' name, Amen.

CHAPTER TEN

A DETERMINED PATH TO EASTERN ILLINOIS UNIVERSITY

Chapter Ten

A Determined Path to Eastern Illinois Univerisy

Reflection Plan and Seeking Guidance

One night in late July, during my prayer time, I remembered a teacher telling me that I would never go to Eastern Illinois University or graduate with a bachelor's degree. I argued with her, but she simply ended the conversation with, "You won't get in."

In the Fall of 2000, I went back to Lake Land College to give school another try. I had been a total failure my first time around, so I knew this time I had to give it my best. I returned to Lake Land College with a focus on speech communication and broadcast journalism. Growing up in a university town and being told I would never get into the college I had dreamed of since childhood only made me want it more.

Community college wasn't easy for me, so I had to devise a plan for success. I consulted with Steve and Jesse, my bandmates and true friends who were incredibly intelligent. After speaking with Steve and joking around, I decided to pursue television and radio broadcasting. Lake Land College had a wonderful radio program that provided real, live, hands-on experience. Being a performer in a band and speaking to small crowds made radio broadcasting a natural fit for me and a place where I felt I could succeed.

Acceptance and Breakthrough

By the Fall of 2001, I had pushed through a year and a half of school and finally applied to EIU. After several weeks of anticipation, I received a letter in the mail saying I had been accepted! I was filled with joy and felt overwhelmed that I had finally achieved what others said I would not be able to do because of my ADHD. Being accepted into EIU after being told I never would be, became a significant breakthrough in my life. When I look back, I realize it wasn't just hard work and perseverance that got me there. It was my faith in God.

Bill Johnson, pastor of Bethel Church in Redding, California, once said, "Faith comes from surrender, not striving." How true this was in my life. I gave up my friends and core lifestyle to follow Jesus. I surrendered and trusted that God would lead me down a path to success.

Walking on Sunshine on a Cold Winter Day

By December 2001, with Christmas around the corner, my mind was fixed on moving out of my parents' house and living on the EIU campus. For the previous semester, I had left First Assembly of God in Mattoon, Illinois. It was my home, where I came to know Jesus and where my band had started out. Leaving was a difficult choice, but I decided to attend the Christian Campus House (CCH) at EIU. I loved going there, where I built lifelong friendships with wonderful people. CCH also had student housing, so that Christmas, I asked my parents if they could help me live there for the Spring semester. My Christmas gift that December was them saying, "Yes, you can live there, and we'll pay the rent." This was a life-changing moment for me. Finally, I was going to live on my own. The thought of being a college student living around campus, eating in the nearby dining halls, and walking to class became a reality.

A Determined Path to Eastern Illinois University

In January 2002, my first day living at EIU was finally here. I woke up, got ready, and as I brushed my teeth, I could hardly contain my excitement. I grabbed my coat and bag and headed out the door to walk to class. As I walked down 4th Street and passed the sports complex buildings on the left, I looked up at the bright, sunny sky. The wind cut through my coat, and my face felt so cold, but I was too excited to care. I was filled with joy and said to God, "Thank you for everything." I was almost in tears. To this day, I still cannot find the words to explain the incredible grace of God that overwhelmed me. I had accomplished what seemed impossible—I was an EIU student living on campus and attending my first class. I was walking on sunshine that cold, winter day.

Early College Years and Adaptation

As I reflect on my academic journey at Eastern Illinois University from 2002 to 2006, and my prior years at community college, I often kept my course load between 9 and 12 credit hours per semester. Living on my own, playing in a band, and attending university wasn't easy while managing ADHD. Still, I found that adaptability and quick thinking helped me adjust. Broadcast journalism especially honed these skills by giving me hands-on experience with camera equipment, where I could explore creative shots and work on sports and news packages.

I loved the field because it allowed me to dive into editing, shaping my ability to craft narratives and stories. Stories have always played a significant role in my life, even in video games, where I gravitated toward role-playing games (RPGs) with rich storylines that pull you in.

Storytelling and Creative Projects

Stories can have deep historical roots. In the era of Jesus, they served as powerful tools to demonstrate God's power and share the testimonies of the resurrection. Back then, the Bible wasn't yet a consolidated book, and many relied on manuscripts from the Old Testament. Storytelling among early Christians built their faith and inspired me to appreciate stories' profound impact on people.

This affinity for storytelling was one reason broadcast journalism felt like second nature to me. I could create stories through writing, filming, or narrative construction. Even with my band, I would think about the show's overall structure and how to captivate the crowd beyond the music. We would add theatrics and interactive elements to tell a story, even if the plot wasn't immediately clear.

In 2003, my band recorded our second album, adding short skits to connect the songs into a cohesive narrative. Jesse, Steve, and I crafted scripts, developed our own Foley art (sounds created from objects or environment), and incorporated a story. Though not universally well-received, I loved the creative process, and to this day, I still enjoy the memory of building those stories.

Academic Growth and Challenges

During my academic career, I sought out classes where I could write papers, deliver speeches, and weave narratives. It was a natural fit in broadcast journalism because storytelling was a requirement. However, as time passed, I realized that camera work wasn't the path I wanted as a career. I transitioned to corporate and general communication, though my major remained broadcast journalism when I graduated.

Tests, quizzes, and endless assignments, particularly in the sciences, presented challenges. I opted for a Bachelor of Arts rather than a Bachelor of Science because science demanded concrete results and proven theories, while I thrived in writing papers or delivering polished presentations. Although I struggled in these classes, I passed them and found enjoyment in the process.

One standout course was psychology, which I took in a large lecture hall with an engaging professor. When I struggled with multiple-choice tests, he worked with me and offered a revised test with more writing opportunities. Despite containing some true/false and multiple-choice questions, this test format aligned better with my skills, and I managed to pass the course.

Even now, memorizing information for tests that may never apply feels burdensome. This mindset traces back to grade school, where I resisted learning topics that didn't interest me. For information to resonate, I needed hands-on involvement and immersion in the creative process, pioneering my own path through education.

In the early 2000s, computers and laptops were becoming increasingly necessary for writing papers. Although I had a desktop computer and later a laptop, I often wrote by hand, particularly for narrative storytelling. My professors wanted handwritten papers, at least for my journalism and English classes, and it felt more natural to me.

Meeting My Future Wife

September 2003 marked the end of an era as my band, The Saints, neared its conclusion. My bandmate Jesse was set to move to California on September 7th to pursue his education in animation. We were in the midst of wrapping up our second album, and had dedicated the entire summer to this project, playing gigs and immersing ourselves in the creative process. One fateful day, September 6, 2003, we performed our last show together as a band (though we did manage to reunite for one more gig in 2005). That last night, we released our second album—a significant milestone that felt like the perfect goodbye.

The dissolution of the band hit me particularly hard. It became challenging to relate to friends who hadn't been part of that musical journey. I had a few acquaintances from the Christian Campus House at college, yet I was combating deep-seated feelings of rejection that had haunted me since my younger years, even though I believed I was following the right path with Jesus. During this phase, I found myself slipping back into old drinking habits, though fortunately, this relapse was brief.

Shortly thereafter, I found myself at a fall retreat organized by the CCH, which had gathered about 80 attendees, many of whom were new students. We got there late on a Friday. The retreat kicked off with some worship, followed by small group discussions. I positioned myself at the back of our overcrowded room, feeling hesitant to participate because of the personal challenges I had been facing recently.

As we were making our introductions, I couldn't help but notice a freshman named Meagan. She shared about the struggles she faced and her aspirations to represent Christ on her basketball team. Her honesty and openness touched me deeply, prompting me to voice some encouragement to her in front of everyone. Later that evening, I asked her to join me by the campfire for a relaxed conversation. Her cousin, who was also in attendance, tagged along. I played the guitar as we all spent the time getting acquainted with one another.

Despite feeling a profound connection with Meagan, I found myself hesitating to ask her out. My band had recently disbanded, and I was grappling with personal and spiritual challenges. I was stuck in a rut—neither actively living out my faith nor sliding back into old, destructive habits. When they announced the imminent demolition of the Christian Campus House apartments to make way for a new building, I made the decision to move back home earlier than I had originally planned. This move led me to distance myself from some friends and reassess my social circle.

Once back in the comfort of my childhood home, I poured my heart out to my mom about the deep ache I felt from the band dissolving and the profound void it left in my life. After all, the band was an integral part of me for nearly four years. I also shared my resolve to make better decisions and to press on with my college education. Despite the weight of my sorrow, I brought up the fall retreat which brought a flicker of curiosity to my mom's eyes. When she inquired if anything positive had resulted from that experience, I found myself speaking of Meagan, a remarkable person I met there. I recalled to my mother how Meagan's authentic soul and steadfast faith had truly caught my attention.

It was December 2003, and the semester had just wrapped up. I was delivering pizzas for a local restaurant. As I was leaving Lincoln Hall, where many of the student-athletes resided, I bumped into Meagan. She was a basketball player and had to stay on campus over the holiday break, just like many other athletes whose seasons were in full swing. As I headed out, she caught sight of me and called out my name. Seizing the moment, I awkwardly but sincerely asked her on a date, and to my delight, she agreed. We started dating and continued throughout college, which eventually evolved into marriage. This relationship, conceived during a challenging period of my life, emerged as a pivotal foundation for my personal and spiritual growth.

The English Professor

Before I graduated, I needed to collect a few of my writings for a required portfolio. Without digital backups, I called my English professor from English 1002, the toughest in the department, to see if she had any of my papers. She warmly invited me to her office and shared, "I've kept every single one of your writings."

This surprised me, as I never thought a professor would hold on to everything I wrote. She told me, "Jake, you're such a talented and beautiful writer," showing me examples of my work. Despite never giving me higher than a C, she explained that it was to challenge me because she saw potential I hadn't recognized in myself.

She continued, "Every paper I returned to you was covered in red ink because I wanted to push you to your fullest potential. I knew you could rise to the challenge if I didn't let you settle for less." She believed strongly in her ability to spot exceptional talent. "You are such a powerful writer, and I know talent when I see it," she said, encouraging me to put off graduating and switch my major to English.

Sitting across from her, I could sense her genuine belief in my abilities as she revealed her reasons for keeping my work. "You were the toughest professor I had at the university," I admitted, "but you inspired me to conquer these challenges and do it for myself."

She encouraged me to keep writing, saying that God had given me a talent for storytelling and that I should use it. Her words were both a validation of my abilities and a call to action. She recognized in me a gift for writing that I had yet to fully embrace. I considered what she said but thought to myself, "Yeah, that's not in the cards for me."

Even with the struggles, I ultimately passed all the required courses, and although my GPA wasn't perfect, the growth I experienced in college shaped me beyond the classroom. Learning to tell stories, deliver speeches, and craft narratives was foundational in finding my rhythm in life.

College Graduation

It was December 2006, a pivotal month that marked the culmination of my academic journey. After years of struggle, resilience, and hard-fought victories, I stood on the brink of a milestone that some thought I would never reach—I was about to graduate from Eastern Illinois University. As I waited for my turn to walk across the stage, a flood of memories washed over me. I remembered the skepticism of a teacher who once firmly stated that I would never be able to attend, much less graduate from Eastern. Sitting there, ready to prove her wrong, I felt a surge of mixed emotions, but I knew that my success was not just my own—it was also thanks to those who had stood by me.

My journey was significantly shaped by influential figures like my 8th grade science teacher, who always had faith in my abilities, and my college

English professor, who recognized and nurtured my writing skills. My parents, particularly my mom, had been my biggest supporters from day one, advocating for me and ensuring I had the resources to succeed. My dad had imparted crucial life lessons that went beyond the classroom.

I also thought about Meagan, my girlfriend and a 4.0 student who excelled in academics and basketball. Her disciplined approach to studies had a profound impact on me. We even took a class together, and I remember, with a chuckle, that one time I outscored her on a test—a small victory we still joke about.

On graduation day, as I walked across the stage, I shook hands with Lou, the president of Eastern Illinois University. Lou was not just an administrator but a family friend; his wife, one of my favorite high school teachers, had always encouraged me. Receiving my diploma from him felt like a validation of all the hard work and the challenges I had overcome.

After the ceremony, I found myself back in the arms of Meagan and my family. Pulling my mom into a gentle embrace, I murmured, "Mom, I did it. I graduated from Eastern Illinois University." It was a moment of sheer victory, a powerful declaration against the doubts and labels that had haunted me for so long. Tears welled up in both our eyes, and I just held her tighter than ever before. I then looked over to my dad and gave him a big hug. In that moment I felt the weight of attaining a college degree fall from my shoulders.

The joy of graduation was intertwined with thoughts of my future with Meagan. Back on July 4, 2006, I had proposed to her at the giant cross in Effingham, Illinois, a landmark by the intersection of interstates 57 and 70. She had said yes, and as we walked away from the graduation venue, I was filled with anticipation and gratitude. Holding her hand, I thanked her for her support and looked forward to our life together. "I can't wait to marry you," I said, reflecting on our journey and the path laid out before us.

That day, as I thought about the twists and turns of my life, I was profoundly grateful for every challenge and every supporter. My graduation was not just a personal achievement; it was a victory for everyone who believed in me, and a testament to the power of faith in Jesus Christ and perseverance.

Getting Married

The date was June 2, 2007, and I was moments away from walking down the aisle. The anticipation was palpable as I prepared to marry Meagan, the woman I knew was destined for me. Surrounded by my closest friends from my band and college, who were all part of the wedding, I adjusted my tie and approached my dad and brother. My brother, always my stalwart supporter, was my best man, just as I had been for his wedding. Choosing between him, Jesse, Steve, and Bob, all groomsmen, had been a difficult but heartfelt decision.

A profound, wordless embrace with my dad conveyed everything—no words were necessary. Our shared hug spoke volumes of the journey to this moment. I then proceeded to ascend the stairs to meet Roger, my pastor and mentor from Christian Campus House, who would officiate our wedding. Walking down the aisle, I was greeted by the sight of numerous friends and family, some of whom I hadn't seen in ages, as well as significant figures from Meagan's life, including her basketball team and coach.

As I stood on the grand stage, waiting for Meagan to walk down the aisle, I pondered over the commitment we were about to make. In that instant, a lifetime of thoughts passed through my mind, centering on the durability of our union. I felt a profound gratitude to God for the blessing of Meagan's presence in my life, reflecting on how different things might have been if not for that transformative, rainy day in November 1999 when God reached out to me.

The ceremony began, and one by one, the groomsmen and bridesmaids made their way down the aisle, each an important part of our lives. I felt especially grateful for Jesse, Bob, and Steve, who had significantly shaped my journey with ADHD and personal growth. Their companionship had been instrumental in molding me into the person I had become.

When the music paused and everyone rose, it was Meagan's moment to walk down the aisle. The sight was breathtaking. I felt the Holy Spirit's warmth and saw a radiant light enveloping her as she walked toward me. Her father gently handed her over to me, and as our hands met, I could see and feel her emotions mirrored by my own nervous tremors.

The exchange of vows was deeply emotional, culminating in the eagerly awaited pronouncement, "You may kiss the bride!" Wedding bells rang and we began to walk outside to take our first ride as Husband and Wife. As our chauffeur drove us around, I looked into Meagan's eyes and said, "I will love you to the moon and back!"

Key Takeaways

1. **Overcoming Doubt with Determination:** Despite being told by a teacher that I would never attend or graduate from Eastern Illinois University, I proved that with perseverance, faith, and the right support system, one can defy expectations and achieve their dreams. This serves as a powerful reminder to readers that external doubts should not define one's potential or limit one's achievements.

2. **Power of Supportive Relationships:** Throughout my journey, I highlight the significant impact of supportive relationships—from my bandmates who helped refine my academic focus, to my girlfriend Meagan, whose influence helped me stay on track academically. This underscores the value of having positive influences and mentors in overcoming life's hurdles, especially for those dealing with ADHD.

3. **Faith as a Guiding Force:** My faith plays a crucial role in my life decisions and achievements. By surrendering my doubts and fears to God, I find the strength to pursue my goals and make significant life changes.

4. **Embracing One's True Self:** The story reflects on the my journey of self-discovery and acceptance, particularly in how I embrace my ADHD as part of my identity rather than a limitation. My story encourages readers to accept and value their unique traits and challenges, viewing them as strengths that can lead to personal growth and success.

Personal Reflection

- **Facing Doubt:** Think about a time when someone doubted your abilities or when you doubted yourself. How did you respond to these challenges? Reflect on what strategies or mindsets helped you overcome these doubts. How can you apply these lessons to current or future challenges?

- **Role of Supportive Relationships:** Evaluate the relationships in your life. Who are your mentors, friends, or family members that have positively influenced your path? Consider reaching out to thank them or think about how you can be a supportive figure in someone else's life.

- **Influence of Faith:** How does faith influence your decision-making and daily life? Whether it's spiritual faith or faith in your abilities, reflect on how this has shaped your experiences and resilience. What can you do to strengthen or reassess this aspect of your life to better align with your goals and values?

- **Embracing Individuality:** Consider the aspects of your personality or life that you may have viewed as setbacks or challenges. How can you reframe these to see them as unique strengths? Reflect on steps you can take to more fully accept and utilize these traits in a positive, empowering way.

Interactive Journal

Overcoming Obstacles:
- Write about a significant challenge you have faced and overcome. What did you learn, and how did it shape your outlook on future obstacles?

The Role of Supporters:
- Reflect on the support you have received during difficult times. How has this support influenced your journey, and how can you offer similar support to others?

Faith and Life Decisions:
- How does your faith or core beliefs guide your decisions? Describe a time when your faith provided direction during a crossroads moment.

Future Aspirations:
- What are your aspirations for the next few years? Set specific goals for personal growth based on the lessons you have learned so far.

Prayer

Dear Heavenly Father, Thank You for the paths You have guided me through, for every hill and valley that has shaped my journey. As I reflect on my own experiences and the story shared in this chapter, I am reminded of Your constant presence and steadfast love.

Lord, I ask for Your continued guidance as I navigate the challenges and opportunities ahead. Help me to recognize Your hand in every part of my life, guiding me toward Your will. Grant me the resilience to overcome obstacles, drawing strength from Your word and the examples of those who have walked before me.

Please continue to surround me with supportive people who encourage and uplift me. Let me also be a beacon of Your love and support to others, sharing the grace You have so generously given me.

As I plan for the future, imbue me with wisdom and clarity. Help me to align my goals with Your purpose, ensuring that my actions reflect the values You have instilled in me. And in moments of doubt or difficulty, remind me of Your past faithfulness, that I may find confidence and peace in Your promises.

Thank You for Your unending love and for the gift of life's journey. May I walk each day with courage, knowing that You are with me, guiding and protecting me.

In Jesus' name, Amen.

CHAPTER ELEVEN

STARTING FRESH

Chapter Eleven

Starting Fresh

A New Beginning

By July 2008, Meagan and I had celebrated our first wedding anniversary. She was passionate about advancing her education and opted to pursue a master's degree in kinesiology at Eastern Illinois University. Over that year, I found myself oscillating between various jobs, doing whatever was necessary to keep us afloat. From delivering ice cream to quaint rural towns to laying concrete on expansive commercial sites and painting the weathered walls of apartment buildings, I did it all.

As Meagan neared the completion of her master's degree, I felt the weight of a decision pressing on my heart. Charleston, my birthplace, no longer felt like home, especially after dedicating my life to Jesus; it seemed mired in memories of a person I no longer recognized. One quiet evening, I sat down with Meagan and shared my restlessness.

"I think we should consider moving," I told her gently, watching her reaction closely. Charleston, with all its familiar streets and faces, suffocated me with reminders of my past self. Meagan looked surprised but curious. "Where to?" she asked. "Champaign, IL," I responded, a place I hoped would offer us both a fresh start. Her practical response immediately went to logistics: "How are we going to afford this move?"

I didn't have all the answers yet, but I felt a conviction that it was the right step. "I'll find a job there," I assured her, "Whatever it takes for us to start anew."

In the early 2000s, my father had embarked on constructing several upscale homes in Champaign. Through his work, he had come to know a variety of business owners and successful entrepreneurs, one of whom was the head manager of a large car dealership in Urbana, IL. Eager to dip my feet into the world of car sales, I asked my dad if he could introduce me to the man. With a nod, he agreed, saying, "Sure, let me reach out to him first and I'll let him know you'll be calling."

My father contacted me soon after we spoke. "Hey, you're in the clear. Go ahead and give him a call." I hesitated, holding the phone, pondering what words to muster. As I dialed the number, my mind raced, 'What am I going to say?'

The gentleman on the other end answered, and I introduced myself, "Hi, my name is Jake Hickenbottom, and my dad is Jim Hickenbottom." To my surprise, he was already anticipating my call. Without a hint of surprise, he responded, "I hear you're looking to sell cars. Why don't you report to work for me next week on Monday?"

In that moment, a sense of excitement washed over me. I was speechless, gripping the microphone tightly. Mentally, I was already celebrating, pumping my arm in the air as I exclaimed silently, "Yes!" Out loud, I managed to say, "I will be there. What time do you want me there?" He replied, "We start our day at 7:00 am." With the call concluded, hope and excitement for this new beginning swelled within me.

As the days melded into weeks, I found myself embarking on the relentless commute between Charleston and Champaign, where I had started selling cars at a Toyota dealership in Urbana. The long drives began to wear me down, not just in spirit but also financially, as I watched my gas money dwindle with little income to show for it. One evening, I turned to Meagan and suggested, "Maybe it's best if I stay in Champaign for a couple of weeks while you wrap up your master's, and then you can come join me." She nodded in agreement, acknowledging the practicality of the idea. However, the looming question remained—where would I stay during that time?

I reached out to my old friend Steve Letner, the lead singer and guitar player of my band, The Saints. During our time apart from the band, Steve had married Shelby, our trumpet player, and they had started a family with two children. They also lived in Urbana, not far from the dealership where I was working. As we talked on the phone and caught up, I explained my situation to Steve. I told him I needed a place to stay for a few weeks, maybe even a month or so, until we could find a place to live and get settled in Champaign. He talked things over with Shelby, and they agreed to let us stay with our dog in their backroom connected to the back of the house. It wasn't the biggest area, but it suited our needs, and we were grateful.

Several weeks flew by, and Meagan completed her master's degree. Graduation day arrived, but the thrill of celebrating was tempered by the immediate need to pack up our apartment and relocate. Moving into Steve and Shelby's house was relatively smooth yet accommodating the routines of two distinctly different families under one roof proved to be a genuine challenge. Nonetheless, it was a learning curve about understanding and cooperation. Having traveled extensively with Steve and Shelby, sharing hotels and guest homes, our dynamic seemed to work well enough. However, introducing an additional dog, two kids, and Meagan into the blend was more demanding than anticipated. Despite the challenges, things somehow fell into place. We were incredibly fortunate to experience their generosity, and eventually, we secured a new place to call our own.

Selling Cars ... Not For Me

Meagan and I had just settled into our new apartment condo. Everything seemed to be moving along smoothly, yet a growing unease shadowed my days, stemming from my job in car sales. Despite the successful sale of a brand-new truck on my very first day, subsequent opportunities to seal deals became increasingly scarce. The commission-based pay structure, particularly unreliable during the economic downturn of 2008, only compounded my struggles. Keeping up in this field and trying to make a decent living became an insurmountable challenge as the industry faced widespread difficulties.

As I mulled over my career options, I found myself puzzled about how to utilize my broadcast journalism degree without working at a news station. During one of my discussions with a close friend, he proposed an idea: "Jake, you're pretty handy with computers. Why not consider a job in IT?" I hadn't thought of that possibility before, but it resonated. I frequently visited a place called Computer Deli in Champaign, a tech haven I often ventured to from Charleston just to explore the latest gadgets and ponder potential upgrades for my own computer setups. Over numerous visits, I had formed a good rapport with Andy, the store manager. The thought struck me, "I could work here. It would be an ideal steppingstone into an IT career."

After I submitted my application, Andy assured me he would be in touch soon. True to his word, he called within the hour to offer me the position. I expressed my need to provide a two-week notice at the Toyota dealership as a courtesy to the individual who had employed me. Upon completing my notice period, I commenced my new role at Computer Deli.

Reconnecting With My ADHD Doctor

As the months rolled by, my job at Computer Deli turned into a remarkable experience. I forged new friendships, picked up a wealth of knowledge from Andy, and honed my skills in selling and assembling computers. Yet, amid these successes, one challenge persisted—maintaining focus and attention at work. This struggle stemmed from my decision to stop taking my ADHD medication a couple of years into college. I had managed to complete my degree without Ritalin during the latter half of my studies. Opting out of medication during college was tough, but I was determined to navigate my academic responsibilities unaided. It was a crucial point in my life; I believed that learning to adapt without medication would significantly benefit my future.

In the world of IT, I quickly discovered just how crucial focus and meticulous attention to detail could be, especially when faced with multifaceted issues. As my knowledge of the field deepened, the complexities seemed to multiply. Andy, who had taken on the task of mentoring me, often became exasperated. My constant desire to inject a bit of fun into our sessions clashed with his approach, as I struggled to stay focused and absorb the intricacies of what he was diligently trying to teach me.

In October 2008, Meagan started a new chapter as a cardiovascular technician at Carle Hospital. This opportunity not only marked a pivotal turn in her career, but also reinstated her access to medical benefits. By early 2010, encouraged by this newfound stability, I made the decision to get in touch with my ADHD specialist and resume my medication regimen.

As time marched on, I reconnected with the doctor who had originally diagnosed me with ADHD. With his guidance, I resumed medication, bracing myself that Monday morning with the familiar yet distantly remembered stimulant coursing through my system as I headed to work. Everything felt a bit surreal, acclimating to a medication I hadn't taken in years, but the adjustment was surprisingly smooth.

The workday kicked off with Andy guiding me through some complex tasks. Within an hour, I was approaching him with the completed work in hand. His initial response was a dubious one, "Yeah, right." However, after scrutinizing my efforts, his skepticism melted into approval. "You actually completed everything, and it's done very well," he remarked. Noting my unusual quietness, he added, "You're extremely quiet this morning." I couldn't help but let out a slight chuckle as I confessed, "I'm back on my ADHD medication." His immediate reply brought a rare, warm glow to my heart, "Let's keep you on that, lad."

Advancing My IT Career Path

By the time 2011 rolled around, I had spent two and a half years at Computer Deli. It dawned on me that I had soaked up all the knowledge and experience the place could offer, compelling me to seek out a more professional realm in the IT industry. This resolve steered me through a variety of jobs, as I searched for the one that truly resonated with me. My journey took me from a professional IT firm that serviced small businesses to a helpdesk role at Carle Hospital, and ultimately to a substantial position at a major insurance company in Bloomington, Illinois. Each step, with its own set of challenges and learning curves, slowly but surely shaped my career path.

As my career progressed and my salary increased, I found myself earning a substantial amount of money at a rapid pace. Being child-free and witnessing the rise in my income, I chose to embrace a lifestyle that, in hindsight, was somewhat unrestrained. One of my perennial challenges, whether under medication or not, has been my struggle with ADHD, particularly with impulsivity and a tendency to make decisions without thorough consideration. With ample financial resources at my disposal, I became a member of the Urbana Country Club, purchased two new vehicles, and engaged in careless spending, never pausing to think about saving.

In 2014, my tenure at the large insurance company ended when they scrapped the project I was hired for and, consequently, my services were no longer required. Anticipating this, I had already reached out to a friend working in the telecom industry, who graciously offered me a position to keep me afloat while I searched for something more permanent. Thankfully, by late 2013, I secured a role at a rapidly growing company that specialized in constructing cell phone towers, as well as maintaining and inspecting cell towers. The job was exhilarating, and it presented an exciting new chapter in my career.

As my career was advancing, so was Meagan's. In December 2013, she completed her nursing degree, a feat she achieved while working at Carle Hospital. Earlier in the year, she had started as a nurse in the Heart and Vascular Institute at the same hospital. That pivotal year, as our professional lives flourished, we were also preparing for another major event—Meagan was pregnant with our first child. Our conversations often circled back to finances, contemplating whether we could manage expenses like being a part of a country club or maintaining payments for both a car and a truck. Despite the looming uncertainties, my response was consistently affirmative—yes, we could handle it.

Becoming a Dad

It was early July when the contractions began. My wife was on the brink of bringing our first child into the world. Like any expectant young couple, we hurried to the hospital amidst a flurry of nerves and excitement. That night, amongst chaos and the soft hum of the hospital lights, Lily was born. The moment the doctor placed Lily into my arms right after her birth was transformative. For the first time in my life, as I gazed down at her, I whispered, "This is my child. I'm now a dad." When I cut the cord, it felt like I was sealing my new identity as a father.

After Meagan and Lily had been given the all-clear, we settled into a hospital room for the night while the doctors made periodic checks on both mother and daughter. Throughout this time, I found myself cradling Lily, gazing at her tiny features, and continuously thinking to myself, "I'm finally a dad."

As the days rolled on, we made our way back home. We began setting up Lily's room, settling into the semblance of a new routine. With my return to work looming, a different weight settled on my shoulders. Each morning, as I headed out, Meagan's words echoed in my mind, "Can we afford this?" The reality of additional costs started to dawn on me—childcare, clothing, and potentially even more if we were to have another child. For the first time in my life, I approached my finances with a newfound sense of responsibility. It was time to stop digging myself deeper into debt and start building a more secure future for my family.

Becoming a father was an incredible experience. I cherished those moments cuddling with Lily in my rocking chair, as we both drifted into sleep. Yet, it often felt as though, sooner or later, Lily would need to return to her mother's embrace. Meagan would reassure me that as Lily grew, our bond would strengthen. While it was difficult to accept at times, I understood that, for now, Lily's needs were closely tied to her mother.

The Writing on the Wall

It was now October 2015, and my career at the cell phone tower company was going well. However, my health started to take a different turn. I began noticing white patches in my mouth that would never heal. These patches started forming persistently, causing significant discomfort. I sought medical help often, which resulted in considerable time lost at work.

The company I was working for was in a decline after expanding too quickly. It reached a point where I was processing numerous terminations daily, and I saw the writing on the wall. Despite the company's struggles, I had nothing negative to say about my experience working there. But the fear of losing my job began to set in.

Due to budget constraints, the company was looking for any way to cut costs, including letting go of personnel for the smallest reasons. I eventually found myself speaking to my boss about my medical situation, explaining how no doctor could provide a proper diagnosis. He informed me that I had used up all my paid time off hours and could not continue taking time off work to see doctors. As I walked out of his office, I felt terrified.

The following week, I had to call in sick to see a doctor. The white blisters in my mouth had become so severe that I could not eat. That afternoon, HR contacted me, arguing that my reason for seeing the doctor was not valid. During that conversation, the HR Director offered me a severance package. With no other option, I had to accept it, as it would provide some financial stability for a bit longer.

Facing Rejection and the Pursuit of a Diagnosis

Losing my job and running out of money really weighed on me. We were forced to surrender our car to the bank and ended up buying a run-down vehicle just to have a second mode of transportation. We chose to keep the truck since it had lower payments and retained more value.

The money had all run out, and we were surviving on a single income. I severed ties with the country club and sold many possessions that I never thought I'd part with. It seemed like every day I was doing something to clean up the financial mess I had created.

Throughout my period of unemployment, I diligently searched for new job opportunities. Despite my persistent efforts, each rejection email ending with "sorry, we hired someone else" intensified my sense of defeat. Several months passed in this manner, and as my hope dwindled, the stress manifested physically, resulting in more painful white blisters in my mouth. Despite hitting this low point, I refused to surrender to despair. My perseverance finally paid off when I secured a position at a software research company in Champaign.

It was November 2015, and I stood on the threshold of a new beginning. As I brushed my teeth that morning and kissed Lily and Meagan goodbye, I paused for a moment to offer a silent prayer of gratitude for the opportunity that lay before me. The painful blisters in my mouth had finally subsided somewhat. After consulting numerous doctors, I had been prescribed oral steroids to tackle the inflammation—these seemed effective, though the relief was often short-lived. But that day was different; not only was I starting a new job, but I had also been upfront with my new employers about my health condition, explaining that I might occasionally need to consult medical professionals or seek treatment until a definitive diagnosis could be reached.

As I stepped into my new role, it wasn't long before I realized I might be out of my depth with some of the tasks expected of me. Having been out of work for a while, I threw myself into mastering the diverse IT systems and processes. The company's operational approach was unfamiliar, especially their use of software and operating systems. Noticing my struggles, my boss took it upon himself to frequently meet with me and guide me through the intricacies of Linux, the operating system I was familiarizing myself with. Throughout my career, I had primarily relied on Windows-based systems; although this wasn't my first encounter with Linux, it was my inaugural experience managing systems operated by it.

As time passed, I honed my skills to proficiently execute all the necessary tasks assigned to me. Gradually, everything began to fall into place. I was part of the sole team in the company tasked with the round-the-clock monitoring and management of critical systems. Thus, it came as no surprise when I was chosen to handle the night shift. I was the new guy, and everyone wanted the daytime shifts.

As I adjusted to the night shift, I began to notice that my tongue was becoming blistered, just like the rest of my mouth. I remember one night a part of my tongue felt like it simply peeled away in my throat. The pain was excruciating, and I immediately sought medical attention. I was quickly prescribed oral steroids again to manage the condition. However, my doctor also decided to perform a biopsy of my tongue to analyze the condition more thoroughly and examine a sample.

Later that week, I found myself sitting apprehensively in the surgical chair of the center, as my oral surgeon prepared to remove a small portion of my tongue. As they strapped me down and made their preparations, I blurted out a question fueled by both fear and a desire for truth. "Is this going to hurt?" My surgeon met my gaze and replied honestly, "I'm going to be honest with you, this is going to hurt." While his honesty was appreciated, panic started to rise within me and I quickly proposed an alternative, asking if instead they could take a part of my cheek that had the same issue.

Before I could receive a response, I felt the sharp sting of several injections numbing my tongue. I had endured numerous shots in my mouth through the years, but this was the first ever to pierce my tongue. The pain was excruciating, and with my inability to scream, it magnified, making it the most torturous experience I had ever withstood. Finally, the biopsy ended, and all I wanted was to go home and weep out the pain and fear for hours.

After two long weeks of waiting, I finally received the results, and I was diagnosed with Pemphigus Vulgaris.

Pemphigus Vulgaris

Pemphigus Vulgaris is a rare, autoimmune disorder that causes blistering and erosions on the skin and mucous membranes. It occurs when the body's immune system mistakenly attacks the proteins in the skin and mucous membranes, leading to the formation of painful blisters. Here are some key points about Pemphigus Vulgaris:

Symptoms:

- **Blisters and Erosions:** Painful blisters on the skin, often starting in the mouth.
- **Fragile Blisters:** Blisters are fragile and can break easily, leaving open sores.
- **Pain:** The sores can be very painful and may lead to difficulty eating or swallowing if they occur in the mouth.

Causes:

- **Autoimmune Response:** The body's immune system produces antibodies against desmoglein, a protein that helps keep the cells attached to one another.
- **Genetics:** There may be a genetic predisposition to developing Pemphigus Vulgaris.

Diagnosis:

- **Physical Examination:** Initial evaluation of blisters and sores.
- **Biopsy:** A skin biopsy can be performed to examine the cells under a microscope.
- **Immunofluorescence:** A test that uses antibodies to detect the presence of autoantibodies in the skin or blood.

Treatment:

- **Corticosteroids:** Oral corticosteroids like prednisone are commonly used to reduce inflammation and immune system activity.
- **Immunosuppressants:** Medications like azathioprine or mycophenolate mofetil may be prescribed to suppress the immune system.

- **Biologic Therapies:** Rituximab, a monoclonal antibody, has shown effectiveness in treating Pemphigus Vulgaris.
- **Pain Management:** Analgesics and other supportive care to manage pain and prevent infections.

Prognosis:

- **Chronic Condition:** Pemphigus Vulgaris is often a chronic condition requiring long-term management.
- **Complications:** Without treatment, it can be life-threatening due to infections and fluid loss from the open sores.

Good News and Bad News

During my early days at the new software research company, I encountered a myriad of surprises. From tackling fresh IT challenges to adjusting to the night shift, and even mastering an entirely new operating system—each day set its own course. However, nothing could have prepared me for the biggest revelation that was yet to come.

One crisp November evening in 2015, shortly after starting my new job, Meagan and Lily joined me for pizza at a cozy restaurant near my workplace. We settled in, savoring the warmth of freshly baked pizza, when, as I was about to take my last bite, Meagan cleared her throat. "I have something to tell you," she said. Curious, I responded, "Sure, what's up?"

"I'm pregnant," she revealed.

Her words caught me completely off guard, prompting me to blurt out, "Are you serious?"

With a reassuring nod, she confirmed that she was indeed expecting. A wave of joy and overwhelming emotion crashed over me; this was the last news I had expected to hear that evening. According to the doctor, our new addition was due in late August of the following year.

As the initial shock subsided, excitement began to bubble within me. Our quaint family of three was about to grow. I couldn't wait to welcome this unexpected blessing, expanding our little family to four.

As the sonogram later revealed, we were having a boy. When I first heard the news, joy and excitement washed over me. Additionally, there was the thrill of having a son to carry on the family name, especially since my brother had only fathered two girls at that point. However, as time passed, my brother's family expanded with the adoption of Parker and the birth of Liam. It was incredibly thrilling to now have boys in the family, breaking the pattern after a stretch of only having girls.

August 2016 was waning, and I was wrapping up my third shift when the first shift started trickling in. I took a moment to remind my boss about discussing my paternity leave with HR as my son's birth was imminent. Agreeable, he suggested we head to the HR office on the 6th floor together. As we walked into HR, I was struck by a sense of preparedness in the air, as if they were expecting me. They gestured for me to sit down. I was puzzled, wondering if they knew what I was coming to speak to them about or if it was something else.

Then, the HR director began to speak. "Jake, we are terminating your position as of today. Your services are no longer required. You may file for unemployment or seek another position within the company when one becomes available," she announced. Those words hit me like a physical blow. Overwhelmed, I felt tears brimming in my eyes. There I was, on the cusp of one of the happiest moments of my life, and suddenly, I was losing my job. Words evaded me at that moment; all I could do was sign the paperwork laid out before me.

The elevator ride down with my now ex-boss was painfully awkward. He admitted, "I didn't know how to break it to you." Barely holding myself together, I replied, "I'll collect my things from HR tomorrow. I need to go home." The reality of my situation weighed heavily on me as I walked out, the future uncertain and more daunting than ever.

As I drove home, tears streamed down my face, and I found myself shouting to the heavens, asking, "Why, God? Why?" In desperate need of support, I reached out to Meagan, knowing she was already at work. I pleaded with her to step away from her responsibilities momentarily because what I had to share was grave. When she could talk, I choked out the words that my job was gone, eradicated from the company's structure. It's a conversation etched forever in my memory.

In the deafening silence that followed inside my truck, I wrestled with a dreadful thought: How could I possibly tell my wife, just a week before our son was due, that his daddy had just lost his job? But as we spoke, I managed to tell her about the severance details — my accrued time off being cashed out, getting one last paycheck, and the possibility of filing for unemployment.

We made a pact then, a decision to hold off the worries until after our son's arrival. We promised each other we'd navigate through this uncertainty together, after we'd had time to celebrate our new beginning as parents.

Although my wife and I had decided to wait and see how things unfolded once our son was born, I found myself facing a painful decision—I needed to sell my truck. It was a gut-wrenching feeling I will never forget. We had only a year and a half left on the payments for the beautiful 2013 Toyota Tundra. I didn't want to part with it but being out of a job left me with no alternative. At that point in my life, it felt as though I was gaining a son but losing everything else. My health was deteriorating, I lost the truck I cherished, and my job was gone; it seemed like my world was turning upside down. Yet, ironically topping this turbulent time like whipped cream and a cherry was the blessing of welcoming our second child.

The Birth of my Son

The day had finally arrived, and the contractions began. I quickly grabbed my phone and called my mother, nervously saying, "Hey, can you come to Champaign? I need someone to watch Lily—Meagan's going into labor." Without hesitation, my mom agreed, reassuring me with a prompt, "I'll be there as soon as I can." It wasn't quite time to head to the hospital yet, which fortunately gave us enough time for my mom to make it here. After what felt like the longest hour, Mom arrived, and with relief washing over me, Meagan and I made our way to the hospital.

All the anxiety and worry I had been harboring about losing my job and relying solely on unemployment benefits simply vanished. In that moment, I made a conscious decision to fully immerse myself in this incredible experience with my wife, knowing it was a memory we would cherish for the rest of our lives.

The moment arrived when Lincoln was born into our family. Even though Meagan held him first, I had the privilege of cutting the umbilical cord. As things settled down, I cradled Lincoln in my arms for the first time. As I gazed down on my newborn son, I made a promise—one that he couldn't understand but one that would forever anchor my purpose. "I will always take care of you as long as I am alive, and I will always love you," I whispered. Those words were not just a vow to him but a kind of closure for the turmoil in my life. They marked a profound realization: I was responsible for this new life, and I was committed to do whatever it takes to uphold my promise.

A few hours after Lincoln's birth, I reached for my phone and excitedly called my mom, "Come over and meet your grandson, and bring Lily too!" As Lily entered the room, our eyes locked and a mutual understanding passed between us—this was a precious moment. "Come meet your new brother," I whispered softly to her. As she looked at Lincoln for the first time, I sensed a bond forming, one that I knew would be unbreakable. It's also worth mentioning that from that moment on, I find it nearly impossible to separate the two.

Election Night 2016

On November 8, 2016, a pivotal day unfolded in the United States: it was election day for the presidency. I found myself headed to The Vineyard Church of Central Illinois in Urbana, not just to fulfill my civic duty but also to seek solace during a turbulent period in my life. Although the primary reason was to cast my ballot, the visit inadvertently steered my life in a new direction—both politically and personally.

Stepping into the church, I was instantly reminded of how long it had been since I last crossed the threshold of a house of worship. As I exited the voting area and entered the church lobby, I was greeted by the sight of several church staff members busily working on the auditorium stage. A profound realization dawned upon me: my soul was yearning for spiritual guidance, especially as I grappled with the Pemphigus Vulgaris I had been battling.

Compelled by this newfound desire, I met with the executive pastor. Together, we retreated to a quiet corner of the building to engage in prayer and conversation. With sincere hearts, we prayed for divine healing from my affliction. As our dialogue continued, I opened up about the struggles I was facing in my professional life as well.

Perhaps driven by a mix of faith and desperation, I inquired if I could assist with the auditorium's stage remodel. Clearly taken aback by my unexpected request, the pastor asked why I was offering my help. I shared that I was a Christian without a church home, and without current employment, I was eager to contribute and find purpose. Graciously, he accepted my offer, marking the beginning of my regular attendance and involvement at the church—a decision that has since enriched my life.

Trip to Northwestern

It was December 27, 2016. My mother and I were navigating the wintry streets to Northwestern Hospital in Chicago, Illinois. Anyone acquainted with Chicago during the frigid embrace of December knows the bite of its cold. Truthfully, I was dreading the chilly gusts, but I understood the importance of our journey.

Upon our arrival, we parked the car in the hospital's garage and made the brisk walk across to the main building. I was on the verge of meeting one of the top dermatologists, a specialist in Pemphigus Vulgaris. Back home, my condition was a puzzle for local doctors—none had the experience or knowledge required for my case. My rheumatologist had thus pointed us toward this expert at Northwestern.

Little did I know back then, merely three specialists worldwide were deeply familiar with Pemphigus Vulgaris. Reflecting on it now, I feel a deep sense of gratitude that our drive was merely two hours north, rather than across the country. This trip, cold as it was, marked a pivotal moment in my journey toward healing.

We had finally arrived, and it was time to check in. A nurse escorted me to the room where I would meet with the dermatologist. After a lengthy wait, the doctor entered the room. Our conversation stretched for about an hour as we explored various treatment options, discussed the specifics of my condition, and outlined the next steps.

At that time, I was on a very high dosage of an oral steroid—a medication typically prescribed in small doses maybe a couple of times a year. Due to this, I experienced a significant weight gain, and my body was suffering and breaking down because of the medication.

I expressed my concerns to the dermatologist as I urgently wanted to get off the steroids. He agreed with my sentiments but also cautioned that I would need to continue the medication a little while longer.

As we delved into the discussion of potential treatments, he introduced the idea of chemo grade infusions designed to manage the flare-ups characteristic of this condition. He mentioned that many individuals who had undergone this type of infusion treatment had eventually gone into remission. However, he was also candid about the severe side effects, some of which could be fatal. By the end of our consultation, he had provided all the necessary information for me to take back to my rheumatologist, who would be overseeing the chemo grade infusions.

I stepped out of the room to find my mother waiting for me, her eyes brimming with questions. "Did you finally get some answers?" she asked. I nodded, feeling a weight lift off my shoulders. "Yes, Mom, I did. It looks like I finally have a viable plan for treating this chronic autoimmune issue." I sighed a little, the rarity of my condition dawning on me again. "Apparently, the chances of someone having it are about one in a million. It's incredibly rare."

The dermatologist was genuinely pleased that I sought him out for treatment. He shared that many medical professionals aren't familiar with this condition or how to manage it, often exacerbating the problem. "He was really glad I came to him," I told my mother. The doctor had also mentioned that although the condition has been present for a long time, it wasn't well-identified or understood. It felt good to finally have some clarity and a path forward after so much uncertainty and pain.

As my mother and I departed from Chicago, we expressed our gratitude to Jesus for guiding us to someone capable of managing my health crisis. In the ensuing months, I regularly met with my doctors and was scheduled for my initial infusion. My levels dramatically improved, dropping into the normal range, only to begin creeping back up after six months. Although I wasn't completely in remission or cured of my condition, the significant reduction in sores in my mouth and the alleviation of back pain brought immense relief. It felt wonderful to be able to enjoy eating again without the agony in my mouth. When my levels started to rise, blisters would reappear in my mouth, prompting my doctors to arrange for another infusion.

Getting My Life Back Together

In the early months of 2017, I was feeling much better and found myself eager to plunge back into the working world. I secured a position at a small IT shop in Decatur, which later led to an opportunity at a nearby private school. There, I taught STEM subjects—Science, Technology, Engineering, and Mathand also handled the school's IT needs. Because I had a four-year bachelor's degree, all that was required of me was a substitute teacher certificate, given that the classes I taught weren't part of the core curriculum.

The school was affiliated with a church on campus, and I took on additional IT responsibilities there to supplement my income. It turned out to be a beneficial arrangement, and I made many lifelong friends. One of my students from those days, who was in the seventh grade at the time, went on to open her own pet grooming shop after graduating. Today, our family's dog is a happy client of hers.

I found myself returning to church full time and engaging more deeply than ever before. Every Saturday evening, I made sure to attend the service, participated in various classes offered, and volunteered in any capacity needed. Slowly but surely, I felt like I was piecing my life back together.

Key Takeaways

1. **Career Transition and Challenges:** I transitioned from various jobs in Charleston to a new career in Champaign. I faced significant challenges, including a struggling economy, lack of job satisfaction in car sales, and eventually finding a fulfilling role in IT, which marked a major turning point in my career path.

2. **Health and Personal Struggles:** I experienced severe health issues, notably Pemphigus Vulgaris, an autoimmune disorder. My journey included dealing with misdiagnoses, multiple doctor visits, and painful treatments. Ultimately, I found relief through specialized medical care and treatments.

3. **Financial Hardships and Adjustments:** I faced financial difficulties, including job loss and the necessity to sell valuable possessions like my truck. These challenges forced me to reevaluate my spending habits and make significant lifestyle adjustments, including leaving the country club and cutting down on unnecessary expenses.

4. **Family Growth and Joys:** Amidst the professional and personal struggles, I experienced profound joy with the birth of my children, Lily and Lincoln. The growth of my family brought a renewed sense of purpose and determination, influencing my outlook on life and my approach to responsibilities and finances.

Personal Reflection

- **Reflecting on Career Transitions:** Think about times when you faced significant career changes. How did you handle the uncertainty and challenges? What steps did you take to ensure a smooth transition, and what did you learn from those experiences?

- **Health Challenges and Perseverance:** Consider a period when you or a loved one faced a serious health issue. How did it affect your daily life and mindset? Reflect on the coping mechanisms and support systems that helped you navigate through those tough times.
- **Financial Struggles and Adjustments:** Reflect on a time when you had to make significant financial adjustments. How did you prioritize your expenses and make difficult decisions? What lessons did you learn about managing finances and setting priorities?
- **Family Growth and Responsibilities:** Think about the impact of major life events, such as the birth of a child or a significant change in your family dynamics. How did these events reshape your responsibilities and your outlook on life? How did they influence your personal growth and relationships with your family members?

Interactive Journal

- Reflect on a significant transition in your life. What were the emotions and challenges you faced, and how did you navigate them? How did your faith guide you through this transition?
- Think about a major career decision you've made. What were the challenges and uncertainties you encountered, and how did you overcome them? What lessons did you learn that you can share with others going through similar experiences?

Prayer

Dear Heavenly Father, Thank you for the journey and the lessons learned along the way. As I navigate new beginnings and face challenges, may I always find my strength in You. Guide me with Your wisdom and help me to trust in Your plan. Bless my endeavors and my family, and may I always remember that with You, I can overcome any obstacle. In Jesus' name, Amen

CHAPTER TWELVE

FROM CHAINS

TO FREEDOM

CHAPTER TWELVE

FROM CHAINS
TO FREEDOM

Chapter Twelve

From Chains to Freedom

School of Kingdom Ministry, Fall 2017

It was the fall of 2017 when Meagan and I made the decision to delve deeper into ministry. Filled with anticipation, we both applied and were accepted into the School of Kingdom Ministry. Attending weekly classes transformed my perspective immensely. It was a profound exploration of identity, healing, deliverance, evangelism, kingdom theology, and the workings of the Holy Spirit.

The curriculum was meticulously broken down into sections. The initial weeks introduced us to worldviews, followed by intriguing topics like kingdom theology, and identity. It was during this period that I first crossed paths with Putty Putman. Putty was an extraordinary instructor, having earned his postdoctoral degree in physics from the University of Illinois. Yet beyond the world of academia, he felt a divine calling to be a pastor and a teacher, eventually starting the School of Kingdom Ministry which was now in its seventh year.

One of the unique teaching methods at the School of Kingdom Ministry was quite experiential. It pushed us out of the conventional classroom setting to practically apply what we learned. This meant venturing into public spaces to pray for the sick, participating in local outreach programs, and learning to uplift and encourage our fellow believers. This hands-on approach was both challenging and incredibly fulfilling, allowing us to live out the teachings of Jesus in real-world situations.

When I first encountered the teachings on identity, they struck me so profoundly that I felt compelled to revisit the manual and rewatch the weekly videos recorded for remote campuses, seeking deeper understanding with God's guidance. Putty presented it in such a unique and practical way that I came to truly grasp what Jesus accomplished for me on the cross—that I am a new creation. Through both semesters at the School of Kingdom Ministry, my understanding of my own identity deepened. I began shedding aspects of my life that no longer served me, reaching a point of comfort and self-acceptance. As I did, I started to recognize the extensive damage I had inflicted upon myself over the years—facing rejection from peers and struggling with ADHD, while grappling with anger and frustration for not fitting into society's prescribed mold. It became clear that these experiences did not define me; they were not my identity in Christ.

One of the segments of the course that deeply resonated with me was the unit on relationships. In this unit, Putty and his brother Dan explored what it means to live according to God's desires for us, emphasizing love over fear and control. This was a transformative lesson for Meagan and me, as it shed light on new ways to nurture our marriage.

Being someone with ADHD, I've noticed that relationships can sometimes turn sour. The intensity of my character and personality can be overwhelming for someone who doesn't fully grasp or cherish my unique traits, potentially making their presence in the relationship strained. In the context of a lifelong commitment like marriage, it's unrealistic to expect perfection at all times. Yet, a solid foundation is crucial, particularly when ADHD is in the mix.

During the course, I became acutely aware of how often I defaulted to control during conflicts with Meagan. My past had shaped a version of me that sought to dominate, a version at odds with my true self. Recognizing these tendencies marked the beginning of a gradual yet essential transformation. To this day, as I am writing this book, I continue working on relinquishing these old habits.

With each step taken to remove these outdated responses, I see a noticeable improvement in my relationship with my wife. Such incremental changes have increasingly brought us closer, enhancing the love and understanding between us.

The dynamic Meagan and I share has significantly shaped my perspective on parenting. I aspire to create an environment in which our children can witness and learn from our embodiment of love and respect, as aligned with God's relational paradigm. Although I have faltered countless times, not always demonstrating the pinnacle of love towards my family, I remain committed to refining my approach and doing better. It's crucial that our children observe and absorb our actions—how we live responsibly and what we welcome into our lives. Among the most profound decisions is our commitment to keeping our Christian life active, continuously involving ourselves and our children in church activities, a practice that remains steadfast to this day.

Integrated Healing Lab

It was now late February 2018. Meagan and I had just wrapped up our first semester immersed in both schooling and ministry, and we were deepening our involvement in our church. At the School of Kingdom Ministry where we were enrolled, we were introduced to the integrated healing model, a holistic approach that embraced physical healing, emotional-inner healing, spiritual healing, and deliverance. An annual highlight of this coursework was the Integrated Healing Lab. During this lab, our class would gather in the chapel room where a person would sit in the center chair, encircled by a small group of classmates. The group leader would then step forward to minister to the seated person, aiming to put our newly learned theories into practice.

In that quiet space in a large chapel room, I found myself seated, vulnerable yet open, as the group leader began to pray over me. As he asked me questions, delving deeper into my emotions, a consensus slowly formed amongst everyone present. They sensed unforgiveness in my heart. This realization struck me with such force; I had indeed been harboring resentment toward many who had wronged me. I was resentful, not just because of my ADHD, but because of the myriad of miscommunications and misunderstandings that life invariably brings.

The journey of forgiveness began then, moving from one person to the next that has hurt me. But the pivotal moment came when I confronted my feelings toward my father. My love for him was undeniable, yet I needed to forgive him for the struggles inherent in our relationship; for the frustrations of raising a child with ADHD. It was no easy task for him, and equally, I needed to forgive myself for the strain I had imposed on him, for the times I reacted poorly.

As I forgave him and forgave myself, a physical reaction overwhelmed me—I trembled and collapsed to the floor, tears streaming uncontrollably, intermixed with sobs. It felt as though a massive weight, long carried, was lifting. Rising to my feet, lighter, something transformative began within me, revealing who I was through Christ.

I handed my burdens over to God, my deep-seated unforgiveness. And as I did, I felt a profound shift. "Here, take these ashes," I said, finding peace in surrender, hopeful for what lay ahead, healed and wholehearted in my renewed spirit.

That night, Meagan was absent. I believe Lincoln was unwell, but I had to fetch Lily, so I walked across to another section of the church to pick her up and then returned to the integrated healing lab as things were wrapping up. Lily was gleefully dancing on the stage, engaging playfully with another adult in the group, as I approached Putty. He began inquiring about recent events, and I opened up about my experience with unforgiveness and the immense relief I felt afterwards. The conversation soon shifted to my autoimmune condition, Pemphigus Vulgaris. I'll never forget what Putty said next. "Jake, I often find that those with severe autoimmune issues struggle with loving themselves." In that moment, as I met Putty's gaze—Putty, who was gradually becoming a friend—I was struck with a realization that had never dawned on me before: I did not love myself.

This revelation hit me like a ton of bricks—spiritually, mentally, emotionally. It became overwhelming. I reflected on every aspect of my life until that moment, understanding why I had often treated others poorly. It was because I didn't love myself, and unconsciously, I treated them the way I treated myself, without even realizing it. Moreover, linking my autoimmune disease to this lack of self-love simply astounded me.

Putty asked if he could pray for me. "Yes, of course," I responded. As he laid his hands on me and began to pray, a tension built up inside me, a controllable yet forceful tension. Anger surged within me, and a deep internal pain began to manifest. It was difficult to describe fully what was happening, but I knew this was not of this world. Something spiritual was occurring, manifesting through me. Call it what you want, but it felt like a deliverance.

As Putty continued to pray, I found myself collapsing to the ground, clutching the carpet. I couldn't fully see or control what was happening. Amidst this chaos, I remember shouting to Putty, pleading for him to take my daughter away from the scene. As I lay there on the ground, my grip gradually loosened, and clarity began to return to my mind. The last thing I recall from that profound moment was Putty invoking, "Jesus, more Holy Spirit, Jesus," over and over again.

As I reflected on my long conversation with Putty, I came to a stark realization: I had been harboring feelings so intense, they had rudely intruded into my life, taking control without my conscious awareness. It was in that moment I recognized this invasive force as a spirit of rejection. A part of me still felt its lingering influence, a sign that I had a long journey ahead on the path of forgiving. This was only the first round of a much longer battle.

SOKM Graduation

May 2018 arrived, and with it, graduation day for the School of Kingdom Ministry. It had been a challenging journey filled with profound learning about healing and the joy of forming an amazing new circle of friends. One friendship that blossomed unexpectedly was with the Director, Putty Putman. I felt a divine nudge that I was called to bring more fun into Putty's life—a vision that I received prophetically but kept to myself until much later. Despite my initial reservations, Putty and I started to spend time together. We played vintage video games, explored a variety of fun restaurants, and even took our kids to a children's museum in Indianapolis. This marked the beginning of a friendship I never anticipated, a bond that endures to this day.

As Putty stepped onto the stage and delivered his remarkable speech, proclaiming that graduation day had arrived, we all proceeded in line to receive our certificates of completion. It was followed by a moving ceremony where our Small Group leader offered prayers for us. It was a simple day, yet it marked the beginning of something entirely new. I began to cultivate more friendships. Among those were Putty's brother Dan and his friend John, who both remain in my life to this day.

Having a close circle of friends reminded me of the old days with my band, though this time, it wasn't centered around playing and writing music. It was about growing and experiencing life together. The most significant difference is that while my band eventually disbanded, my new circle of friends—despite living far apart—as of today, still talk, play games online, and make a point to meet up whenever we're in town. It feels as though we haven't missed a beat at all.

The drive home was quite enjoyable, as Meagan and I reminisced about everything that had transpired at the School of Kingdom Ministry. We realized that our lives would never be the same again, and that filled us with hope. No longer would we be the individuals we once were, for we now comprehended what it truly meant to live in Christ. We grasped the transformation necessary to become who we were created to be, relationally as a couple in connection with God as His son and daughter.

Summer 2018 New Lifelong Friends

During my days at the School of Kingdom Ministry, I was fortunate to forge a friendship with Putty Putman. At the time, Putty was navigating some tough waters. Like so many educators, he often found himself stretched thin, juggled between the demands of people needing his attention and his numerous commitments within the ministry. On the other hand, I was immersed in my role as a STEM teacher at a private Christian school, perpetually hunting for innovative concepts to inspire my students. Recalling that Putty held a PhD in physics, I ventured to ask if he could spare some time to brainstorm educational ideas. He warmly accepted.

Meeting Putty outside the familiar environment of ministry was a delightful change, especially since this time our conversation pivoted toward science-themed ideas for my classroom. As we exchanged several innovative thoughts, I couldn't help but notice the sheer joy radiating from him as he discussed potential classroom activities. It suddenly hit me—Putty wasn't just any enthusiast; he was a bona fide scientist, having earned his PhD in physics from the University of Illinois.

As we continued our conversation, a thought crossed my mind: "Could Putty be a nerd like me? Does he indulge in video games just like I do?"

Curiosity got the better of me and I finally asked, "Putty, do you play video games?" His response, "Why do you ask, Jake?" took me by surprise. But in that moment, I felt a nudge from the Holy Spirit, urging me, "Jake, it's up to you to remind Putty how to have fun like a child again. He's missing that in his life, and he needs it." It was a clear sign for me. Seizing the opportunity, I invited him over for a video game night. To my delight, he accepted, and we made plans to turn it into reality.

Putty and I began bonding over our shared childhood passion for video games, a joy only the true gamers could understand or appreciate. My collection was expansive—nearly 2,000 vintage games and about 40 consoles. I still remember the day Putty came over for the first time, bringing along a Kirby game for the Nintendo Wii U, probably thinking my collection was modest. I couldn't wait to show him the real extent of it. I led him to my game room and watched his reaction as he walked in. He had expected a small setup, maybe twenty games at most, but instead his eyes met rows upon rows of games, meticulously organized on shelves I had built myself from 1x2" and 2x4" pieces of wood nailed to the wall as a shelf. He must have stared at that wall for a good 20 minutes, utterly speechless. As he took in the treasure trove my room held, I knew our plans were about to change. That night, Putty realized that we would not have time for Kirby.

After our first game night, Putty shared the fun we had with his brother Dan and several others from our church and the School of Kingdom Ministry staff. The word quickly got around, and soon enough, Putty's friends were reaching out to me, keen to know if I had specific games or consoles, and eager to join our game nights. This excitement spurred us into hosting regular gatherings, sometimes twice a month, where we would play video games and enjoy great food until midnight. Those nights were special; it was during these gatherings that I made some amazing, lifelong friends. Among them was Putty's childhood friend, Andrew, who quickly became one of my best friends. I also grew closer to Putty's brother, Dan, and even became part of his small group. Although many of these friends now live over a thousand miles away, our friendships have remained steadfast, and we still stay in touch regularly.

Pemphigus Levels Rising Again

By January 2019, I had undergone three infusions for Pemphigus Vulgaris. After extensive forgiveness and a deliverance prayer session with Putty, my antibody levels had begun to climb again. The increase wasn't as sharp as before, yet it signaled the need for another infusion. During my prayer time at home, I was graced with a vision from the Holy Spirit, urging me to include my new friends in the upcoming infusion treatment.

The next infusion was scheduled at a cancer center, a place where harsh realities converged. There I was, in a pod, an IV needle in my arm, seated amidst fellow patients battling their illnesses under a barrage of chemotherapy. Despite the center's commendable facilities, the open setting, which exposed me to everyone else's pain and struggle, amplified my discomfort. In this vulnerable moment, I gathered my courage and reached out to my friends, asking them to join me in prayer during the infusion. When I spoke to them, I explained what I wanted prayer for. I wanted prayer that God to bless the infusion, reveal His mighty presence, and hopefully, render this infusion as my last.

Andrew, Tim, and Dan all arrived that day to pray with me. It was a defining moment. At that juncture in my life, my circle of friends had dwindled to a precious few. I attempted to maintain connections with some of my old bandmates, sporadically checking in and trying to coordinate meet-ups whenever feasible. But after Meagan and I got married and relocated, the dynamics shifted. My old friends were busy in their new lives and careers, and Jessie had even moved to California.

The presence of my new friends during such a pivotal experience marked a turning point. They were actively participating in my life in ways that continued to resonate deeply with me today as I write this book.

The Orphan Spirit

During the summer of 2019, I was hanging out with Andrew, enjoying some food, playing video games, and talking about life. As we often did, we indulged in delicious food while discussing deeper topics. That day, our conversation turned to forgiveness and unforgiveness, reflecting on what had happened in the Integrated Healing Lab. Andrew, sensing something from the Lord, pointed out that I still had remnants of the spirit of rejection in my life.

As we talked, Andrew asked, "Jake, have you ever dealt with the orphan spirit?" I was taken aback and asked him what exactly the orphan spirit was. Andrew's response was a pivotal moment in my life, changing everything. He explained that while I had forgiven people, I hadn't dealt with the lingering effects—the emotions and feelings left behind. He said, "Jake, when you forgive someone, you also need to forgive them for the way they made you feel. This is crucial because it frees you from the bondage of rejection, pain, guilt, shame, anger, and bitterness. It sets you free."

Feeling like Andrew was my own personal Gandalf from Lord of the Rings, always speaking in riddles, I asked him to explain further. He emphasized the importance of forgiving not just the actions but also the emotional impact, which was essential for true freedom.

Reflecting on our conversation, I decided to develop a plan to address the orphan spirit. As I embarked on this journey, God revealed that this was the key component at the center of all my physical, relational, and emotional problems, as well as my relationship with Him. Previously, I had only cleaned up the "front porch" through forgiveness, but never the "house" itself.

On my hour-long drives to and from work, I began to forgive people again, but this time also forgiving them for how they made me feel. Each act of forgiveness made me feel lighter and more free, helping me to love myself for who I truly was. After about a week, I couldn't think of any more people to forgive. I finally felt truly free.

Putty's Dream and Jake vs Rejection Spirit Round Two

In May 2019, I was wrapping up the school year and preparing to leave my teaching position. I loved being a schoolteacher, but I also missed working in IT. Although I did a lot of IT work for the school, it wasn't the same. I had recently accepted a position at Birkey's in Champaign. Birkey's is an amazing company, and as I write this book, I still work there and love it.

While cleaning up my classroom, I received a call from Putty. "What's up, Putty?" I asked. He began to share some exciting news. Someone had reached out to include him in a documentary about the intersection of science and God. I congratulated him and asked, "What's that got to do with me?" He laughed and replied, "It has everything to do with you, Jake. I want you to be part of the documentary, to be interviewed about your autoimmune issue and the journey you've been on." I agreed, excited about the opportunity to share my story.

Several months later, in mid-November 2019, the filmmaker, Eric—an awesome guy—arrived to start filming. We discussed various aspects of my autoimmune issue, the journey I had been on, the spirit of rejection, and the experiences in the Integrated Healing Lab. After filming, we went to a local pizza restaurant for Chicago-style deep dish. As we got to know each other, I shared my book journey with Eric. We spent the time talking about our respective journeys in film, broadcasting, and storytelling.

As lunch ended and we were leaving, Eric turned to me and said, "Jake, I have a prophecy for you. I really feel this is from the Lord." Intrigued, I said,

"Okay, let's hear it." He said, "Jake, your book on ADHD is not only going to be a light for those who have it, but it's going to change the world's view on ADHD for those who read it." His words were a confirmation of what God had spoken to me about my book.

Eric was in town for two days. On the first night, Putty had a dream. He woke up in the middle of the night, feeling strongly that we should finish the deliverance we started at the Integrated Healing Lab, and that it should be filmed with Eric. The next morning, Putty called to explain his dream. Initially, I was terrified of doing anything like that on camera. Putty reassured me, saying, "Think it through. It's your choice. I'm not going to push it on you." Before the call ended, I knew this was God at work. I said, "Putty, let's do it. I don't care what happens. I just want to be free."

On the following afternoon, November 15th, Eric set up his camera equipment and microphones in a private room at the church. He explained, "I'm just going to leave the camera running. You have this much time. If we run over, I'll find a way to keep going with the batteries I have." I sat down next to Putty, and he asked, "Are you ready?" I replied, "Let's do this."

I laid my hands out, and Putty placed his hand on my forehead. Putty invited the Holy Spirit to be the center of the prayer session. In that moment, it felt like I entered a deep sleep. I didn't even know what room I was in. With my eyes closed, I felt the presence of Jesus. He walked me through all the rejection I had let go of and embraced me in a hug. Jesus reassured me that the spirit of rejection had no power or authority over me anymore. All my autoimmune problems and health issues, fueled by anger, rage, guilt, shame, and my lifelong struggles with ADHD, were being lifted.

It felt like an eternity, but it was only a few seconds. I began to feel intense emotions and started coughing violently from my gut and not my throat. I collapsed to the ground, but in that moment, I was free. I quickly stood up, fully aware of where I was. It felt like I had been at war for 30 years, yet it had only been a few seconds. The video lasted just a couple of minutes. I looked at Eric and asked, "Did you get that on film? Both Putty and Eric were caught off guard by my question, as if what had happened was almost an act—but it wasn't. It was real. God, Jesus, and the Holy Spirit had a hold of me since November 2, 1999, and they hadn't let go. The spirit of rejection over my life was gone and I was finally free.

Finally Free!

Several weeks passed since that day I journeyed into a room with a filmmaker and a pastor—the day the spirit of rejection got its butt kicked. That day, I danced with Jesus on holy ground, proclaiming my freedom.

As of today, while finishing this book, my antibody levels have never spiked like they used to. I've only had a couple of infusions since then. My relationships have improved, and my interactions at work have gotten better.

I started a new journey of learning how to live without the spirit of rejection. Even now, as I write this book, there are moments when I sense rejection creeping in, tempting me to go down that familiar path. But I always stop myself. I choose not to partner with it. It may take a few minutes or even a day, but I always remember what it did to me, and I want no part of it ever again. That's what it means to be free in Christ, to be a new creation. Jesus heals. He is still here. He's not bound to heaven. He's on this earth, speaking to us through the Holy Spirit, guiding us through His word. Jesus is my best friend. Out of all my friends, He is the top. I speak with Him every day, and I'm so thankful for all He did in my life.

I will never argue with anyone that it was the infusions that helped me. They did help me a lot, but my levels always spiked or rose months afterward. Today they do not, and my levels are in remission. Today I am learning to live the way Jesus wants me to live, in His relational paradigm. Never again will I think that having ADHD makes me a failure or that I am something broken that needs to be fixed. For me, ADHD is a gift. I embrace it. I love being ADHD.

As I close this book, I want to say to you, the reader: If you have ADHD, God wants to meet you in it. He wants to teach you how to be relational with Him through it, to do things others can't, to have more energy and abilities than any other mindset on the planet. He wants to use you to pioneer something new and change the world with Him. Don't waste it. Don't go your whole life saying, "I have ADHD, and I'm a problem." Partner with the Holy Spirit. Learn to better yourself through ADHD and look to it as a gift and master the challenging mindset it takes to be amazing.

If you or a loved one is seeking answers for ADHD, I hope you have a better understanding of divergent thinking, hyperfocus, and how the Holy Spirit can guide someone with ADHD. It's not you, the parents or loved ones, who change the person. Your ADHD loved one can only change through God. It's His right, and only through Him will your loved one master the way they were created to be.

I encourage you to be like my mom—a fighter by their side. Lift them up when they're down, like my dad did. Keep pushing them to be a better version of themselves. Never judge them, don't criticize them, but empower them to make good decisions and leave the rest to God. Trust God in it. If you're thinking, "That will never work," I want to tell you that you're wrong. It worked for me, and I'm living proof of God in my life and how He can change it. Mastering ADHD is not a quick fix, it's a lifelong journey.

My final words are these: If you have not accepted Jesus Christ into your heart as your Lord and Savior, now is an opportunity—in a book, of all places. All you have to do is say,

"Jesus, I acknowledge that You died on the cross for me and my sins. I now accept You into my heart. Transform me into a new creation. Jesus, I acknowledge

that I am now right with God, that righteousness is now attained. I will live my life to serve You, Your church, and the world around me. I will take the light up to the mountain and shine it for all to see. I cannot do it alone; with Your help and guidance, there's no stopping me. I will never be the same again. Thank You for meeting me here. I will follow You for the rest of my days. Amen."

REFERENCES

American Psychiatric Association. (2013). *Diagnostic and statistical manual of mental disorders: DSM-5* (5th ed.). American Psychiatric Publishing.

Beaty, R. E., Benedek, M., Kaufman, S. B., & Silvia, P. J. (2015). Default and executive network coupling supports creative idea production. *Scientific Reports, 5*, 10964. https://doi.org/10.1038/srep10964

Children and Adults with Attention-Deficit/Hyperactivity Disorder (CHADD). (n.d.). *Is ADHD related to creativity?* Retrieved from https://chadd.org/attention-article/is-adhd-related-to-creativity/

Crosta, P. (2022). *The link between creativity and ADHD*. Psychology Today. Retrieved from https://www.psychologytoday.com/au/blog/mythbusting-adhd/202205/the-link-between-creativity-and-adhd

English Standard Version Bible. (2001). ESV Online. Retrieved from https://www.esv.org/

Healthline. (n.d.). *Methylphenidate*. Retrieved from https://www.healthline.com/health/methylphenidate-oral-tablet#dosage

Hupfeld, K. E., Abagis, T. R., & Shah, P. (2019). Living "in the zone": Hyperfocus in adult ADHD. *ADHD Attention Deficit and Hyperactivity Disorders, 11*(3), 191-208. https://doi.org/10.1007/s12402-019-00285-z

Mayo Clinic. (n.d.). *Restless legs syndrome*. Retrieved from https://www.mayoclinic.org/diseases-conditions/restless-legs-syndrome/symptoms-causes/syc-20377168

National Organization for Rare Disorders. (n.d.). *Pemphigus vulgaris*. Retrieved from https://rarediseases.org/rare-diseases/pemphigus-vulgaris/

Putman, P. (2018). *The School of Kingdom Ministry First Year Manual, Third Edition*. Coaching Saints Publications. ISBN 9780989832199.

Verbeeck, R., & Koenig, J. (2023). *Concerta (methylphenidate HCl) extended-release tablets.* Cerner Multum. Retrieved from https://www.drugs.com/pro/concerta.html

Yassa, R., & Yassa, A. (n.d.). *Methylphenidate*. StatPearls Publishing. Retrieved from https://www.ncbi.nlm.nih.gov/books/NBK539896/

Lockman Foundation. (2020). New American Standard Bible (2020 ed.). Lockman Foundation.

Dawkins, R. (2013). Do what Jesus did: A real-life field guide to healing the sick, routing demons and changing lives forever. Chosen Books.

SPONSORS

Image created by Jesse Baumgartner during my time in our band.

I want to say a very special thank you to those who have made this book possible finacially. Words cannot express how greatful I am to have you all in my life.

Aikman's Wildlife Adventure – Arcola Illinois
The Rocke Family
David Fendley

There are so many I would like to acknowledge that helped make this book possible. I thank you from the bottom of my heart. I would like to acknowledge as select few.

Putty Putman
Andrew Janssenn
My Wife – Meagan
My Mother - Jo Hickenbottom
My Father - Jim Hickenbottom
The Vineyard of Central Illinois
Meadowbrook Community Church
My Niece – Teja Hickenbottom
John Ciciora
Dan Putman
Dianne Lamen
Wayne Chang
Bob Putman
Shelly Manning
Kyle Peters
Leah Winchester
Shelby Letner

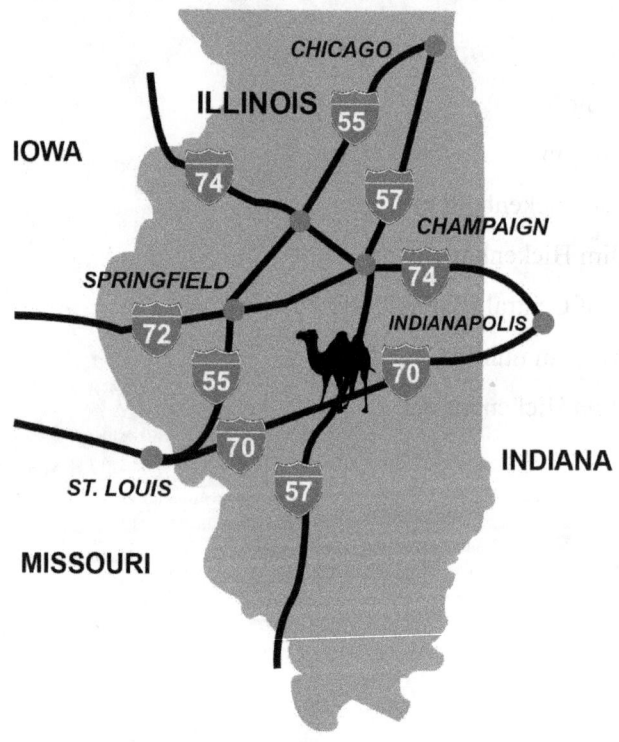

5 MILES WEST OF I-57 EXIT 203
FORMER ROCKOME GARDENS LOCATION
125 N CR 425E, ARCOLA, ILLINOIS 61910

www.ingramcontent.com/pod-product-compliance
Lightning Source LLC
Chambersburg PA
CBHW060655100426
42734CB00047B/1801